A FUNDAMENTAL FREEDOM

A FUNDAMENTAL FREEDOM

Why Republicans, Conservatives, and Libertarians Should Support Gay Rights

DAVID LAMPO

ROWMAN & LITTLEFIELD PUBLISHERS, INC.
Lanham • Boulder • New York • Toronto • Plymouth, UK

Published by Rowman & Littlefield Publishers, Inc.
A wholly owned subsidiary of The Rowman & Littlefield Publishing Group, Inc.
4501 Forbes Boulevard, Suite 200, Lanham, Maryland 20706
http://www.rowmanlittlefield.com

10 Thornbury Road, Plymouth PL6 7PP, United Kingdom

Distributed by National Book Network

British Library Cataloguing in Publication Information Available

Library of Congress Cataloging-in-Publication Data

Lampo, David, 1950–
A fundamental freedom : why Republicans, conservatives, and libertarians should support gay rights / David Lampo.
p. cm.
Includes index.
ISBN 978-1-4422-1571-9 (cloth : alk. paper) — ISBN 978-1-4422-1573-3 (electronic)
1. Gay rights—United States. 2. Republican Party (U.S. : 1854–) 3. Conservatism—United States. 4. Libertarianism—United States. 5. Homophobia—United States. 6. Homosexuality—Moral and ethical aspects. 7. Christianity and politics—United States. 8. United States—Politics and government—2009– I. Title.

HQ76.8.U5L36 2012
323.3'2640973—dc23 2011048982

™ The paper used in this publication meets the minimum requirements of American National Standard for Information Sciences—Permanence of Paper for Printed Library Materials, ANSI/NISO Z39.48-1992.

Printed in the United States of America

CONTENTS

"Mark my word, if and when these preachers get control of the Republican Party, and they're sure trying to do so, it's going to be a terrible problem. Frankly, these people frighten me. Politics and governing demand compromise. But these Christians believe they are acting in the name of God, so they can't and won't compromise. . . . The religious factions that are growing throughout our land are not using their religious clout with wisdom. I'm frankly sick and tired of the political preachers across this country telling me that if I want to be a moral person, I must believe in 'A,' 'B,' 'C,' or 'D.' Just who do they think they are? I will fight them every step of the way if they try to dictate their moral convictions to all Americans in the name of 'conservatism.'"

—Senator Barry Goldwater (R-AZ)

PREFACE

It is an axiom of modern American politics that most Republicans, especially conservatives, are not only anti-gay but also have capitulated to an anti-gay agenda formulated and pursued by the social conservative movement for the past several decades. It's certainly not difficult to understand why that perception is so widely held across the political spectrum and will, if left unchecked, continue to erode support for the Republican Party from independent and younger voters, two voter segments that are particularly supportive of gay rights.

This common perception of Republicans, however, was not always so widely held. It really began in the late 1970s, when Religious Right leaders founded organizations specifically designed to turn conservative Christians into political activists.[1] In 1978, conservative ideologues Paul Weyrich, Howard Phillips, and Richard Viguerie, for example, founded Christian Voice.[2] Reverend Jerry Falwell followed in 1979 with his organization, the Moral Majority.[3] It was a time of great social and cultural upheaval, and social conservatives like these men routinely railed against not just homosexuality and abortion but also what they saw as general moral decay in the country.[4] Although most such evangelicals, as they called themselves, had identified as Democrats (think George Wallace and the Deep South), by the late 1970s they had begun to migrate to the Republican Party in large numbers, eventually coming to wield tremendous power within the Republican Party in primaries and caucuses around the country.[5] The Republican Party platform and pronouncements became more and more explicitly gay-unfriendly as their influence grew. This migration continued into the 1980s, and other large Religious Right organizations, like Pat Robertson's Christian Coalition in 1987,[6] were founded and flourished, in part by drumming up anti-gay bigotry among their other causes.

This Republican hostility to gay rights continued with the now famous "culture war" speech by dark horse presidential candidate Pat Buchanan at the 1992 Republican National Convention. The political columnist and former Nixon administration operative railed against "the agenda Clinton would impose on America—abortion on demand, homosexual rights, discrimination against religious schools, women in combat units. . . . It is not the kind of change we can abide in a nation we still call God's country."[7] His anti-gay invective continued to grow, and during his runs for president in 1996 and 2000, he decried homosexuality as "a lifestyle associated with decadence and national decline" and claimed that AIDS was nature's "retribution against homosexuals," even though by then it was clear that AIDS worldwide was predominantly a disease of heterosexuals.[8] Though most in the Christian Right supported Texas governor George W. Bush for president in 2000, many, perhaps most, of them shared Buchanan's mistaken beliefs about homosexuality and AIDS, and such vitriolic talking points were routinely heard among social conservative activists and leaders in the Republican Party.

In fact, by the 2000 presidential election, more evangelicals considered themselves Republican than Democrat by a 39 to 26 percent margin, a reversal from the late 1980s, when more called themselves Democrats by a 34 to 29 percent margin.[9] The takeover of the Republican Party base by the Religious Right was now complete, with white evangelicals making up four in ten Republican voters by 2006.[10] An emphasis on social issues rather than the traditional economic issues of lower taxes and federal spending had become the norm in the Republican Party. In a year when many formerly Republican voters voted Democrat, 70 percent of self-identified evangelicals still voted Republican,[11] continuing a trend that had existed for at least twenty-five years.

The cultural and political war against gay rights within the Republican Party certainly intensified with the advent of the national discussion, sometimes bordering on hysteria, regarding same-sex marriage that was initiated by the 2003 Massachusetts State Supreme Court decision legalizing gay marriage. That decision turned American society upside down and spawned an intense political and legal backlash from the Right that we are still dealing with today. The Republican Party became downright hostile not just to relationship recognition for gay couples but also to the entire "gay agenda," as it is derisively labeled by many conservatives, including everything from antidiscrimination laws to repeal of state sodomy laws.[12] No measure expanding civil liberties for gay and lesbian Americans was spared their scorn.

President Bush, who early in his administration had surprised his critics and angered his supporters by adopting several relatively pro-gay measures such as a federal employment nondiscrimination policy and nominating an openly gay man as ambassador to Romania,[13] came to personify this general Republican hostility to gay rights by publicly aligning himself with this anti-gay agenda.

In 2004, he began to publicly promote and support measures like the Federal Marriage Amendment at the insistent urging of his social conservative supporters,[14] who had pushed the issue of same-sex marriage to the top of their political agenda. His longtime political advisor Karl Rove devised and carried out a national campaign strategy to turn out social conservatives at the ballot box that year by using the gay marriage issue as a wedge during the presidential election. Voter turnout certainly increased in critical swing states like Ohio as President Bush narrowly won a second term, but political experts still disagree about whether or not Rove's anti–gay marriage strategy deserved the credit for his victory.[15] In the minds of most voters, however, the connection was clear.

That 2004 campaign may have been the high point of the Religious Right's role as kingmaker in the Republican Party, even as it destroyed President Bush's earlier claims that he was a more inclusive Republican. In fact, in almost a mirror image of the evangelical movement into the Republican Party, we saw the flight of millions of moderate and independent voters from the Republican Party over to the Democratic Party,[16] in large part due to the social intolerance promoted by so many in the Republican Party's Religious Right base. The elections of 2006 and 2008 continued that trend, and Republicans took a beating.[17]

The GOP's anti-gay hostility has manifested itself in many ways, from the Republican Party platform's across-the-board opposition to gay rights[18] to anti-gay statements from state and national party leaders and candidates about gay rights and "San Francisco values." Until recently, few Republican candidates or elected leaders bucked this anti-gay agenda, born to satisfy the cravings of religious conservatives and evangelicals whose primary concerns were now with moral issues and "family values" rather than the traditional Republican issues of free enterprise, limited government, and a strong national defense.

As a result, many Americans, including many former Republicans, believe that the party of Lincoln has morphed into a religious party: in the words of former Goldwater deputy press secretary Vic Gold, it has become "the party of God,"[19] a perception shared by millions of American voters, made all the more understandable by the many anti-gay statements and policy proposals put forth in 2011 by most of the Republican presidential contenders leading up to the 2012 presidential primaries and caucuses.

The fact that social conservatives still put their primary focus on social and moral issues rather than economic ones was highlighted at the first Republican Party presidential debate of the 2012 campaign, held on May 5, 2011, in South Carolina.[20] Former Pennsylvania senator Rick Santorum, one of the most outspoken anti-gay candidates running for president, attacked Governor Mitch Daniels of Indiana, who at the time was mulling over a run for the presidency.[21] His crime? He had the temerity to suggest that Republicans put social issues on the back burner and concentrate on the economic issues that voters clearly indicated in the 2010 election were of primary importance. Denouncing Governor Daniels's call for a "truce" on such issues, Santorum said, "Anybody who would suggest we call a truce on moral issues doesn't understand what America's all about."[22]

What a revealing statement by Santorum that was, particularly his substitution of the word "moral" for "social." It reveals Santorum's contempt, shared by many in the Religious Right, for the entire concept of the separation of church and state. In their view, it is entirely proper that government actively promote certain religious values and beliefs while outlawing or controlling the expression of moral beliefs and values they disagree with. Keep in mind then senator Rick Santorum's 2006 statement that the "attack" on traditional marriage posed a greater threat to America than Middle Eastern terrorism, calling the defense of traditional marriage "the ultimate national security issue."[23] By the time Senator Santorum ran for reelection in 2006, the backlash among moderate and independent voters against such extreme views had already begun, and he lost his reelection bid by a whopping 59 to 41 percent margin. Clearly, it is Santorum who doesn't understand "what America's all about."

The aggressive posture of the Religious Right against gay rights intensified as the campaign progressed throughout 2011. In August, the National Organization for Marriage demanded that the Republican presidential candidates sign its pledge not only in support of the Defense of Marriage Act (DOMA) but also to support a federal marriage amendment to the US Constitution to outlaw same-sex marriage nationwide, nominate only federal judges who oppose same-sex marriage, and promise to establish a presidential commission on "religious liberty" that would investigate proponents of same-sex marriage for their alleged harassment of opponents of same-sex marriage.[24] Fortunately, candidates Ron Paul, Herman Cain, Jon Huntsman, and Gary Johnson refused to sign it, but all the others fell in line. Cain joined them in late 2011, perhaps to bolster his "family values" reputation in light of the serious sexual harassment charges that engulfed him just as he was topping some of the polls of the Republican contenders.

Despite the Republican Party's hostility on gay rights, however, a surprising number of self-identified gay and lesbian voters have stuck with the Republican Party in recent presidential contests. Voter surveys revealed that President Bush received one million gay votes in 2000, about 25 percent of the gay vote nationwide, although this support eroded somewhat in the 2004 election.[25] In 2008, 31 percent of self-identified gay and lesbian voters cast their ballots for Senator John McCain and Sarah Palin,[26] despite then senator Barack Obama's very pro–gay rights campaign and Palin's dalliance with certain members of the anti-gay Right, such as James Dobson, late in the campaign. In the critical 2010 congressional election, nearly a third of gay voters supported Republicans.[27]

Although gay Republicans were then (and are today) derided by some (on both the left and right) as an oxymoron, they have in recent years become an increasingly visible part of both the gay and lesbian community and the Republican Party as they fight to change the face of the party. Log Cabin Republicans, the largest and oldest national gay and lesbian Republican organization, has for over twenty years worked to make the Republican Party more inclusive and socially tolerant, while at the same time advancing some of the party's signature efforts, like tax cuts and private Social Security retirement accounts on Capitol Hill. In fact, Log Cabin Republicans had a notable success in December 2010 in helping to repeal the Pentagon's Don't Ask, Don't Tell policy,[28] a historic achievement that will be explored in greater detail later in the book. Without Log Cabin's influence on supportive Republican senators at a critical time in the legislative process, that repeal would never have been realized.

After the resounding Republican defeats in the 2006 congressional election and the 2008 presidential election, the Republican Party was in disarray and turmoil, partly because of the backlash caused by the influence of what Barry Goldwater used to call the "political preachers" and their insistence on using government power to impose their private religious values on the rest of us. While the excesses of the Obama administration and the incredible growth of the Tea Party movement are helping to reconnect the Republican Party to its roots of fiscal responsibility and limited government, many on the right, and in the Tea Party, still share a fundamental misunderstanding of, and even disdain for, gay people and the gay rights movement. Many of them simply misunderstand the goals of the gay rights movement, while many more have fallen for the outrageous lies and distortions about gays and lesbians put forth on a daily basis by the more extreme right-wing organizations and individuals.

As this book will demonstrate, however, there is simply no logical connection between religiosity (and the social intolerance that often goes with it) and the traditional Republican and libertarian values of individual freedom and free enterprise. The anti-gay agenda of the Christian Right succinctly exposes the hypocrisy of those who talk of limited government and individual rights but ignore both when it comes to gay rights and other personal freedom issues. Indeed, it is the defenders of gay rights in the Republican Party, not their opponents, who are keeping faith with the core Republican principles of free enterprise, limited government, and individual rights.

With all the current ferment and upheaval in the Republican Party, now is an ideal time for Republicans and conservatives to learn to think about gay rights in a broader context than simply their own personal religious views, whatever they may be. It is time for them to realize that, in a free society, the highest political virtue should be freedom, not adherence to any specific moral or religious code.

Fortunately, over the past year or two, we have seen signs that many

Republicans, including some elected leaders and candidates, are changing their tune on this issue. In fact, there is a battle going on right now for the soul of the Republican Party, not only over the traditional economic issues most Republicans agree on but also on the issue of making the Republican Party a more socially tolerant and inclusive force for freedom rather than a vehicle for specific (generally intolerant) religious views. This battle has been played out in the Republican Party presidential nominating process, with the candidates representing a broad range of views not just on gay rights but also on their fundamental beliefs about the proper role of government.

This book will examine that battle for gay rights from an explicitly libertarian Republican perspective, making the case for not only why Republicans should embrace gay rights but also why doing so will provide long-term political benefits for the GOP. And it will also show that most rank-and-file Republicans are already far more supportive of gay rights than either the Religious Right or the liberal Left realize or will admit.

The book begins with a brief look at the history of gay rights in this country, in order to put it in the context of other civil rights movements. While the persecution suffered by gays and lesbians may not rise to the level of the slavery suffered by African Americans, the fact is that gays and lesbians have been routinely discriminated against, prosecuted, beaten, harassed, imprisoned, and even killed because of who they are, from the federal level down to small towns and rural areas. The gay and lesbian community has until relatively recently suffered from a widespread and fundamental denial of basic human rights, often quite ugly in how it played out, particularly before the modern gay rights movement was born in the late 1960s.

In chapter 2, I examine the claims of the Religious Right about religious freedom and gay rights and take issue with its declaration that government should be based on "biblical principles." I outline the polling data that show a large and relentless shift away from Republicans by demographic groups once in their corner and also point out the huge disconnect between what social conservatives often preach about "traditional marriage" versus how a large number of them actually denigrate it through widespread divorce and even infidelity. Some social conservatives are in fact shocking in their hypocrisy on the issues of sin and public policy.

In chapter 3, I thoroughly examine the major gay and lesbian issues at both the federal and state levels, including employment nondiscrimination laws for the public and private sectors, federal hate crime legislation, Don't Ask, Don't Tell, state sodomy laws, the Defense of Marriage Act, same-sex adoption, and immigration rights for gay and lesbian partners. I also examine a variety of polls that show a majority of independents and, in most cases, a majority of Republicans are supportive of gay rights on all of these issues.

Chapter 4 tackles perhaps the most controversial of all gay and lesbian issues: same-sex marriage and the passions it ignites on both sides. Perhaps no other issue has aroused such angry reaction in conservative Republican circles as gay marriage, and yet, as polls consistently document, support for both same-sex marriage and civil unions shows undeniable and consistent growth, not only in the general population but also among Republican rank-and-file voters.

With 40 percent of all Americans now living in states with legal same-sex marriage, civil unions, or domestic partnerships,[29] even the Republican Party is quickly changing on the issue of relationship recognition, with the Republican rank and file in particular exhibiting a much more tolerant and politically savvy outlook than most Republican Party officials and legislators, even as a hateful backlash by a panoply of right-wing religious organizations against this increasing tolerance grows ever more intense.

Chapter 5 traces the history of the classical liberal (now called conservative or libertarian) movement in the United States and shows how these two primary strains of thought have clashed at various times in American history, especially in the modern post–World War II era. Those same basic philosophical tensions continue today, not only over issues like gay rights and social tolerance but also on broader issues like the war on drugs, the proper role of government, and foreign policy, among others.

Chapter 6 presents an analysis of the Tea Party that refutes the common public perception that it marches in lockstep with social conservatives on gay issues. Rather, various polls show that about half of Tea Party activists are much more socially tolerant than religious conservatives and far more likely to rate social issues like gay rights and abortion at the bottom of their list of priorities.[30]

Chapter 7 details the rapid changes already taking place within the Republican Party on these issues. With the exception of same-sex marriage, in fact, a majority of Republican voters already supports the so-called gay agenda, a shocking counterpoint to the conventional wisdom on both the left and the right that says otherwise.[31] More and more Republicans are realizing that independent voters, who are critical to the success of Republican candidates nationwide and in many swing states, are uniformly supportive of gay rights, including even same-sex marriage, and that to keep them in the Republican column, the party will have to significantly change its position on gay rights. Quite simply, for both the country and the Republican Party, there's no going back.

Finally, chapter 8 briefly reviews the record on gay and lesbian issues of all of the announced Republican presidential candidates as of this writing and rates their support of gay and lesbian equality. It also presents a frightening glimpse of some of the leading anti-gay conservative organizations in operation today.

As the following chapters will demonstrate, the cultural and political changes that are taking place regarding gay people and gay rights are increasingly rapid. Those who wish to turn back the clock and to force gay and lesbian Americans back into the closet are becoming a smaller percentage of the population each year.

Now is the time for all socially tolerant Republicans, whether conservative, libertarian, or moderate, to speak out and demand that the Republican Party shed its widespread image of intolerance and even hatred toward gays and lesbians by charting a new course of explicit support for equal rights for all, including gay and lesbian Americans. We can have a civil discussion on those issues about which Republicans still disagree, such as relationship recognition and what form it might take, but we have to resoundingly reject the hateful anti-gay prejudice that saturates much of the Religious Right. The future of the Republican Party may be at stake, and it is my hope that this book can play a small part in that ongoing effort to promote a consistent message of limited government and individual rights that embraces all Americans.

1

A SHORT HISTORY OF THE GAY RIGHTS MOVEMENT

Even though many gay and lesbian Americans today face discrimination when it comes to equal rights, it was far worse in the 1950s and 1960s. In those days, gays and lesbians were generally invisible and ostracized if they lived outside the closet. Even in major metropolitan areas, gays lived mostly underground and in the closet.[1] Few commercial establishments served openly gay customers, and even many bars and restaurants that did cater to a gay clientele were owned or operated by the Mafia, which would pay off police in order to operate what were often illegal establishments.[2]

Police were seldom sympathetic to gay victims of assault and other violent crimes, and in some cases, police were actually the perpetrators.[3] Gay establishments were routinely raided by police and were the victims of shakedowns by them to stay in business.[4] Sodomy laws were on the books in the District of Columbia and every state except Illinois, which decriminalized sodomy in 1961.[5] Some convicted of the crime were even sentenced to life imprisonment![6] Gay Americans were routinely characterized by crude stereotypes, even by many in the medical community.

In 1952, for example, the American Psychiatric Association (APA) listed homosexuality as a sociopathic personality disorder, and it was not until 1973 that the APA repudiated its earlier stance.[7] Based on the APA's earlier characterization of homosexuality, twenty-nine states had "psychopath" laws that allowed gays to be detained by the police simply on the suspicion they were gay.[8] According to historian David Carter, in California and Pennsylvania, sex offenders could be confined to a mental institution for life, and in seven states, they could be castrated.[9] Electroshock therapy and lobotomies were sometimes used to "cure" homosexuals throughout the 1950s and 1960s, and "in almost all states, professional licenses could be revoked or denied on the basis of homosexuality, so that professionals could lose their livelihoods."[10]

Known gays were forbidden from working for the federal government, and President Dwight D. Eisenhower formalized this policy of discrimination with an executive order in 1953.[11] The Senate routinely held hearings to investigate how many "sex perverts" worked for the federal government.[12] Between 1947 and 1950 alone, 1,700 federal job applicants were rejected on the basis of such discrimination,[13] over 4,300 were discharged from the armed forces, and 420 were fired from their government jobs for being gay.[14]

The FBI and many police departments maintained lists of known and suspected "homosexuals,"[15] and the US Post Office even kept track of addresses to which gay-related material was mailed.[16] It was not until 1958 in a decision by the US Supreme Court that the right to send gay newspapers, magazines, and other publications through the US mail was reaffirmed.[17] In today's culture, where gays and lesbians are so widely acknowledged and accepted, it's hard to believe such conditions existed for millions of gay Americans, many of them even through the 1970s.

All that began to change in the early morning hours of June 28, 1969, at a small gay bar in New York City called the Stonewall Inn. Located in Greenwich Village and owned by the Mafia, as most such establishments at the time were, it was routinely subjected to police raids and harassment.[18] While today we think of Manhattan as a gay-friendly city, back then the political establishment was hostile and often tried to shut down gay bars by revoking their liquor licenses.[19] Police entrapment and arrest of bar patrons was a routine process.[20]

On that night, however, the usually passive customers of the Stonewall Inn fought back when police arrived to conduct a typical raid and mass arrest. Riot police were called in but had to retreat under a ferocious assault by hundreds of members of the gay and lesbian community who had finally had enough. Over the next several days, thousands of gays turned out to battle police, and the modern gay rights movement was born. Historian Lillian Faderman wrote that "the Stonewall Rebellion was crucial because it sounded the rally for that [gay rights] movement. It became an emblem of gay and lesbian power. By calling on the dramatic tactic of violent protest that was being used by other oppressed groups, the events at the Stonewall implied that homosexuals had as much reason to be disaffected as they."[21]

Although gay rights organizations such as the Mattachine Society and Daughters of Bilitis existed before the Stonewall riot, they took a conservative approach in their battle to win equality. Stonewall led to a new militancy in the gay rights movement, matched by the burgeoning antiwar and counterculture movements. The legacy of that night is reflected in the ubiquitous gay pride rallies and parades that take place every June across the country and the world.

The emergence of out-of-the-closet gays and lesbians continued in the 1970s, and the APA's 1973 decision to remove homosexuality from its list of mental disorders and its call to enact antidiscrimination laws were very influential.[22] Gays and lesbians were moving into the mainstream of American life, but even then, according to Professor William N. Eskridge from Yale University Law School, "lesbians and gay men were not only excluded from service in the armed forces, troops suspected of being gay were subjected to 'witch hunts' by the military police. Sexual minorities were also barred from most police forces and from many civilian jobs, especially in public schools."[23]

In 1971, *All in the Family* became the first sitcom in the country to feature a gay character when one of Archie Bunker's bar buddies came out. The first recurring gay character on TV came in 1972 in the show *The Corner Bar*. Many others have followed, and today gay characters on primetime TV, soaps, and reality shows are routine. In 2010, a study from the Gay and Lesbian Alliance against Defamation said the number of gay, lesbian, bisexual, and transgender characters on TV had reached a new high, with twenty-three gay characters in the year's new season on network television and thirty-five regular gay characters on cable television.[24]

The issue of gay rights was thrust into the national limelight through the effort in 1977 by actress Anita Bryant to organize a repeal of an antidiscrimination law in Dade County, Florida, apparently justifying her efforts on the *Phil Donahue Show* by saying, "The Bible says homosexuals should be put to death and their blood shed over their heads."[25] Outrage against her campaign and its nasty stereotypes of gays led to a boycott of Bryant's well-known employer, the Florida Orange Commission, resulting in a nationwide boycott of Florida oranges. Although her campaign resulted in a temporary repeal of the ordinance, it effectively ended her career and ultimately proved to be a shot in the arm for gay rights groups around the nation.

By the late 1970s, most major urban areas in the country had gay-friendly city governments and had become home to large gay populations—particularly New York, San Francisco, Los Angeles, Philadelphia, and Boston—and gay political power in these cities and elsewhere skyrocketed.[26]

In 1980, the Democratic Party became the first major political party to insert a gay rights plank into its platform, as the Religious Right and its anti-gay agenda became increasingly influential in the Republican Party. Unfortunately, AIDS exploded on the American scene in the early 1980s, and although it spawned sympathy for gays victimized by the disease, it also sparked a growing homophobia within much of the conservative movement, which was reflected by the fact that most elected Republicans opposed almost all pro-gay legislation and did little to contain the growing HIV epidemic.

Nevertheless, gay rights continued to permeate American business and government. In 1982, the *Village Voice* newspaper in New York City became the first business to offer domestic partner benefits, and in that same year, Wisconsin became the first state to outlaw discrimination based on sexual orientation. In 1984, Berkeley, California, became the first city in the country to offer domestic partner benefits to its gay employees.

In 1992, Bill Clinton was elected president after an explicitly pro–gay rights campaign, although his initial effort to allow gays and lesbians to serve openly and honestly in the armed forces resulted in a backlash that brought us the now famous Don't Ask, Don't Tell (DADT) policy that prohibited openly gay and lesbian Americans from serving. At the time, the policy was viewed as a step forward for gay rights because it ended the existing outright ban on gays and lesbians serving in the military. Since the inception of DADT, however, over thirteen thousand service members were forced out of the armed forces due to their sexual orientation.[27]

The year 1993 also marked the first court ruling in favor of same-sex marriage, a shocking concept at the time, even to most in the gay and lesbian community. The Supreme Court of Hawaii ruled that, without a compelling state interest, the state could not bar same-sex couples from marriage without violating its equal protection laws, at the time a radical if compelling legal concept.[28]

In 1998, President Clinton issued the first-ever executive order banning employment discrimination on the basis of sexual orientation for federal employees, a policy with such widespread support that President George W. Bush continued the policy after he assumed office in 2001.[29] And in 1999, California became the first state to enact a domestic partnership law. At the time, it covered only hospital visitation rights, but since then, other domestic partnership rights have been added to it, and the state now offers virtually all of the same benefits to same-sex couples as it does to traditional married couples.

The progress of gay rights has continued at an even quicker pace since the turn of the new century, and the visibility of gays and lesbians has touched every nook and cranny of American life and culture. In 2000, Vermont became the first state in the nation to implement civil unions, a kind of separate but equal alternative to straight marriage on the state level but one that is vastly unequal when it comes to federal marital protections and privileges.

In 2003, the US Supreme Court declared the thirteen remaining state sodomy laws unconstitutional in the *Lawrence v. Texas* case.[30] Although some social conservatives condemned the decision as "judicial activism," libertarian conservatives hailed it as the right kind of judicial activism, grounded in the principles of individual freedom the Supreme Court was meant to protect. Supreme Court Justice Anthony Kennedy, a Reagan appointee, wrote the majority opinion, much of it quite libertarian in its reasoning.

Late 2003 saw one of the most controversial state court decisions ever rendered in *Goodridge v. Department of Public Health*, the Massachusetts case that legalized same-sex marriage.[31] It struck most Americans, including gays and lesbians, like a thunderbolt, completely changing the way millions of Americans looked at marriage. The ruling also sparked a legal backlash at the state level that will take years of litigation and initiative campaigns to undo.

The *Goodridge* decision struck at the heart of the religious convictions of millions of Americans. Both the Bush administration and most of the Republican leadership in Congress moved to exploit the backlash on the right against the *Goodridge* decision through the remaining years of the Bush administration, including a push to pass the Federal Marriage Amendment (FMA),[32] a radical measure designed to preempt the traditional state role in marriage law by setting one federal policy outlawing same-sex marriage for the entire country, regardless of the views of voters and legislatures in states where there was support for same-sex marriage or alternatives to it like civil unions or domestic partnerships.

Fortunately, even in the then Republican-controlled Senate, the FMA never garnered the necessary congressional support to pass.[33] It is considered today to be mostly a dead issue because it strikes at the heart of traditional conservative support for federalism, even on the part of many who oppose same-sex marriage. Consequently, the battles concerning legal relationship recognition for gay couples have played out mostly at the state level, where such issues are better decided in the first place, and that process will continue for the foreseeable future. We will cover those state battles in more detail in a later chapter.

In just over forty years, gays have gone from being a mostly invisible, oppressed minority to one that, while still lacking many basic legal rights, has moved to the front and center of American culture and the political process. There's no going back, and the profound cultural changes that America has undergone will continue at an even faster pace. The following chapters will explain why Republicans, particularly party leaders and elected officials, should stop fighting and start supporting many—if not all—of the legislative and legal aims of the modern gay rights movement.

2

WHY THE RELIGIOUS RIGHT IS WRONG ABOUT THE SEPARATION OF CHURCH AND STATE

Freedom of religion is one of the cornerstones of our republic. Many of the original immigrants to America were fleeing religious persecution in their homelands, and they hoped to establish in the colonies the freedom to follow their own religious convictions free of the supervision of a state church. Such state regulation and persecution was a common phenomenon in Europe and around the world during the eighteenth century, when state power and religious power were often one and the same. Kings throughout Europe more often than not tried to force their particular religious beliefs on the entire population, and religious minorities were often killed or driven from their homes. This routine persecution led in no small way to the religious freedom we take for granted today, because many of those who fled this persecution and came to America were determined to erect, in Thomas Jefferson's words, "a wall of separation between church and state."[1] They explicitly embedded the principle of religious freedom into our Constitution. Generations of Americans have fought and died for this freedom, and it has served us well.

Despite this history, the Religious Right argues that we were founded as "a Christian nation" and should remain one. Beverly LaHaye, founder of Concerned Women of America, is quite explicit about this point. "Yes, religion and politics *do* mix,"[2] she argues. "America is a nation based on biblical principles. Christian values dominate our government. *Politicians who do not use the bible to guide their public and private lives do not belong in office*" (emphasis added).[3]

Religious Right leaders like LaHaye apparently forget that the Founding Fathers deliberately left the words "God" and "Bible" out of the

Constitution, despite their widely held Christian views. As pointed out by journalist Russell Shorto, religious conservatives "who say their goal is to follow the original intent of the founders are ignoring the fact that the founders explicitly avoided religious language in [the Constitution]."[4] While most were deeply religious, the Founding Fathers had often experienced firsthand the consequences of allowing the state to dictate and promote specific religious values, and that played an important role in their efforts to erect that wall Jefferson referred to. That is certainly one reason the House of Representatives specifically rejected during its debate on the First Amendment a Senate proposal that called for making Christianity the official religion of the United States. As Purdue University history professor Frank Lambert concluded, "There would be no Church of the United States. Nor would America represent itself as a Christian Republic."[5] The Founders were quite methodical and very specific about their beliefs regarding the relationship between religion and the state, and their actions make their true beliefs very clear. The young republic had another chance to make its views on this issue clear when the Senate unanimously ratified one of the first treaties to come before it in 1797. Article 11 of that treaty began, "As the government of the United States of America is not in any sense founded on the Christian Religion . . ."[6]

In their book *The Godless Constitution*, scholars Isaac Kramnick and R. Laurence Moore point out that James Madison, our fourth president and one of the chief architects of the Constitution, argued that religious beliefs "are not the object of civil government, nor under its jurisdiction." According to Kramnick and Moore, the Framers wished to enshrine the political principles of libertarian philosophers like John Locke, so they deliberately created "a demystified state, stripped of all religious ambitions."[7]

Many of the Founding Fathers were in fact deists rather than religious in the same way as Pat Robertson, Rick Warren, or other self-appointed spokesmen for the modern evangelical movement. Deists believe the universe has a creator but not the kind of God who rules over the daily lives of human beings with books of scriptures commanding them to act in certain ways. The Founders were instead men of the Enlightenment,[8] the Age of Reason of the seventeenth and eighteenth centuries, who prided themselves on their rationality and freedom of thought. They were the antithesis of theocrats, those who argue that the state should explicitly base civil government on their private religious faith.

In fact, the Founders' contemporaries who believed in the fusion of religion and state (like today's theocrats) often complained about the deliberate efforts of the Founding Fathers to keep the two institutions apart. Those critics agreed with Reverend Timothy Dwight, then president of Yale University, who said the United States had "offended Providence" because we "formed our Constitution without any acknowledgment of God."[9] In 1831, Episcopal minister Bird Wilson of Albany, New York, wrote, "Among all our presidents, from Washington downward, not one was a professor of religion, at least not of more than Unitarianism."[10]

The words of some of our most popular Founding Fathers, in fact, show a very different view of the role of religion and the state than that advanced by modern social conservatives. James Madison, one of the primary architects of our Constitution, wrote that "it may not be easy . . . to trace the line of separation between the rights of religion and the Civil authority. . . . The tendency to usurpation on one side or the other, or to a corrupting coalition or alliance between them, will be best guarded against by an entire abstinence of the government from interference in any way . . . and protecting each sect against trespasses on its legal rights by others."[11] And in 1785, he wrote, "The Religion then of every man must be left to the conviction and conscience of every man; and it is the right of every man to exercise it as these may dictate. . . . This right is in its nature an unalienable right."[12]

Other Founders shared this skepticism. John Adams, our second president, wrote that "the divinity of Jesus is made a convenient cover for absurdity. Nowhere in the Gospels do we find a precept for Creeds, Confessions, Oaths, Doctrines, and whole cartloads of other foolish trumpery that we find in Christianity,"[13] concluding later with the unambiguous belief that "this would be the best of all possible worlds, if there were no religion in it."[14] Those are hardly the sentiments of the modern theocrats we find in the Religious Right.

Thomas Jefferson, perhaps our most famous and beloved Founding Father as well as third president of the United States, wrote in 1802 (while president) that "religion is a matter which lies solely between Man and his God. . . . He owes account to none other for his faith or his worship."[15] He was outspoken in his skepticism of modern religion: "Millions of innocent men, women, and children, since the introduction of Christianity, have been burnt, tortured, fined, imprisoned; yet we have not advanced an inch towards uniformity. What has been the effect of coercion? To make one half the world fools, and the other half hypocrites. To support roguery and error all over the Earth."[16] He later urged his fellow countrymen to "question with boldness even the existence of a God; because, if there be one, he must more approve of the homage of reason than that of blindfolded fear."[17] Perhaps it's no surprise, then, that Jefferson stated that he did "not find in orthodox Christianity one redeeming feature."[18]

And what of George Washington, our first president and the founder of our country? Thomas Jefferson wrote in his private journal that "Gouverneur Morris had often told me that General Washington believed no more of that system [Christianity] than did he himself."[19]

Clearly, the absurd notion explicitly advanced by some on the right (including 2010 Tea Party senatorial candidates Christine O'Donnell in Delaware, Ken Buck in Colorado, and Sharron Angle in Nevada) that the Founding Fathers did not really believe in the separation of church and state simply because they were religious reveals a profound ignorance of what they really said and believed. (Perhaps the outrageous statements by these three candidates questioning the separation of church and state, while everyone else was worried about the economy and out-of-control government spending, were one of the reasons all three were defeated.)

A NEW THEOCRACY?

Today, it is unfortunately no exaggeration to say that many on the right wish to construct their own form of theocracy. They fail to make a distinction between their personal religious beliefs on one hand and civil society on the other, something advocates of freedom have been doing for many years. Some on the right deny they are theocrats, but the *American Heritage* dictionary defines theocracy as "a government ruled by or subject to religious authority."[20] Isn't that exactly what those who demand a government "based on biblical principles" are fighting for?

What better definition of a theocrat is there than LaHaye's definition cited earlier?

One hears self-proclaimed spokesmen for the Religious Right state this belief in different ways. As former congressman Mark Souder (R-IN) put it, "To ask me to check my Christian beliefs at the public door is to ask me to expel the Holy Spirit from my life when I serve as a congressman, and that I will not do." Souder was forced to resign from Congress in 2010 after admitting he had engaged in adultery with a longtime female aide[21] (apparently there *were* times when Representative Souder was willing "to expel the Holy Spirit" during his congressional service). Unfortunately, the hubris and self-righteousness embodied in Souder's statement are widespread among the Religious Right, even those who live in glass houses.

Religious faith is without a doubt deeply embedded in American culture, and it has always played an important part in our history, even in the public square. But "checking one's religious beliefs at the public door," as Representative Souder put it, is exactly what public officials should do when it comes to making laws that seek to force citizens to live by subjective religious or moral codes, at least if they are to remain loyal to the nation's founding principles of individual liberty. To insert one's personal religious beliefs into our laws is to abandon the highest political value of this country, which is individual liberty. This constitutional right to be free from government-imposed religious dogma is what sets us apart from virtually every other nation on earth, and we must fight to preserve it.

Sadly, the sentiments of Souder and LaHaye are echoed by many Republican elected officials and candidates who have bowed to the demands of the Religious Right to bring their faith into public office. Former Arkansas governor and FOX News talking head Mike Huckabee has called for Americans to "take this nation back for Christ."[22] Former Pennsylvania senator Rick Santorum argued at the 2011 Conservative Political Action Conference that "America belongs to God"[23] and that we are all mere stewards of God's gift. Fine sentiments for a Sunday sermon, perhaps, but completely at odds with the philosophy of personal freedom and autonomy the nation was founded on.

When running for president in 2008, then senator Sam Brownback (R-KS) told his supporters that the traditional issues of economic freedom and limited government that defined the Republican Party and its leaders for nearly fifty years weren't enough. "It's the social issues [like opposing gay marriage] first and foremost that drive my passion," he said. "*For me the social issues are why I became a Republican in the first place*" (emphasis added).[24] In other words, while the rest of us have been fighting for the traditional Republican values of free enterprise, individual rights, and limited government, those very same values did not provide enough reason for Senator Brownback to become a Republican. Only the prospect of using the federal government to forcibly instill his religious values on others provided the incentive he needed.

That is a stunning admission and a perfect example of why the Republican Party that once stood for freedom, free enterprise, and limited government is now in the public mind more defined by the religious views of its base than the traditional, more libertarian views of, say, Barry Goldwater or Ronald Reagan, perhaps the two foremost icons of the party in modern times, both of whom explicitly defined their political views as libertarian.[25] In fact, there is no more damning indictment of the negative influence of the Religious Right over the Republican Party than Goldwater's assessment: "When you say 'radical right' today, I think of these moneymaking ventures by fellows like Pat Robertson and others who are trying to take the Republican Party away from the Republican Party and make a religious organization out of it. If that ever happens, kiss politics goodbye." On another occasion he said, "I'm frankly sick and tired of the political preachers across the country telling me as a citizen that if I want to be a moral person, I must believe A, B, C, and D. Just who do they think they are? And from where do they presume to claim the right to dictate their moral beliefs to me?"[26] Senator Goldwater, no doubt, spoke for millions of Republicans and independents fed up with the right-wing control of the party.

It's important to point out that not all Christians have the hubris to presume they have the moral authority to impose their religious beliefs on others. Being a devout Christian, Jew, or Muslim does not necessarily mean you must believe in using government force to impose your personal religious values on unwilling citizens. Even Jerry Falwell once stated that "preachers are not called to be politicians, but soul-winners."[27] That was at one time, in fact, the prevailing belief of evangelicals across the board: one had to find "salvation" voluntarily through a personal relationship with God, not at the point of a gun wielded by a theocratic government.

Although many evangelicals have unfortunately jumped into the political process as a means of spreading their faith, others have not. There is, for example, a growing and vibrant movement of Christian libertarians who strongly believe in the separation of church and state, including on the issue of homosexuality. As Norman Horn of the Libertarian Christians website writes, "Power to regulate personal relationships in any way, including marriage, should never be given to the state. . . . Homosexuals have the same rights as everyone else. . . . Your rights do not change based on your sexual preference." "Though I disagree with a behavior," he said, "I shall not raise an aggressive hand against it. . . . To me, that is the essence of being socially tolerant."[28] Many Christians would argue that this belief represents the true philosophy of their faith.

Doug Bandow, libertarian author of *Beyond Good Intentions: A Biblical View of Politics*, makes the case that "nothing in Christian Scripture indicates that Christians are to capture the state to promote their faith. Rather, it is their obligation to be salt and light, to make their case irrespective of the political regime. Jesus did not preach with the power of the sword. To advocate no government action does not preclude promoting one's Christian views. *It just requires relying on persuasion rather than force*, and that's precisely what the original Christians did" (emphasis added).[29] That is a religious philosophy entirely compatible with the traditional Republican, and libertarian, values of freedom and individual sovereignty.

It is only fairly recently, in fact, that the Republican Party became openly identified with certain religious beliefs and denominations. Most self-described evangelicals used to reside primarily in the Democratic Party and supported Jimmy Carter when he ran for president, but they began to migrate to the Republicans in significant numbers during the late 1970s, a time of both cultural and political upheaval.[30] Everything from the emerging gay rights movement, to the Equal Rights Amendment, to forced racial integration of private and religious schools in the South laid the groundwork for this migration, much of it under the leadership of perhaps the two most famous spokesmen for the Religious Right at the time, Jerry Falwell and Pat Robertson.[31]

Falwell, along with Paul Weyrich, helped found the Moral Majority in 1979, and Pat Robertson was most widely known for his TV show *The 700 Club*, as well as his organization, the Christian Coalition, incorporated in 1987. He has also been known for his numerous outrageous statements about his opponents and claims of divine intervention as retribution for our sinful ways, such as when he blamed feminism for encouraging women "to leave their husbands, kill their children, practice witchcraft, destroy capitalism, and become lesbians."[32] Falwell was prone to similar outrageous statements, blaming 9/11 on divine retribution for America's immorality and tolerance of homosexuality.[33] He eventually apologized for those remarks, but they were remarkably similar to those by Reverend Fred Phelps, the infamous preacher from Kansas who routinely pickets the funerals of dead soldiers with his signs saying they died because America is too tolerant of homosexuality.

Despite these frequent verbal assaults on reason and common sense, millions of evangelical voters (and donors) were motivated into political activism by the sermons and speeches of Falwell and Robertson, among others, reflecting their resentment of the increasingly rapid social change sweeping the nation.

These voters and their allies soon solidified themselves as the new base of the Republican Party. While a plurality of white evangelicals still identified as Democrats in 1987 (34 to 29 percent), by 1996 Republicans out numbered Democrats among evangelicals by two to one, and by 2006, the spread was even greater, 51 to 22 percent, according to polling by the Pew Research Center.[34] While their participation certainly played a part in Republican victories over the past twenty or thirty years, their growing influence also helped lead to the exit from the Republican Party of millions of socially moderate, independent, and self-identified libertarian voters, as well as women and younger voters and others uncomfortable with (or actively opposed to) a party whose agenda seemed to be increasingly "based on biblical principles." This voter shift over several decades has been relentless and unmistakable.

Women voters, for example, routinely voted Republican in the 1970s and 1980s. They broke evenly for Governor Ronald Reagan and President Carter in 1980 but went for President Reagan in 1984 by a 58 percent margin.[35] They split almost evenly again in 1988,[36] but by 1996, President Bill Clinton had clinched 55 percent of their votes.[37] They have continued to vote Democratic ever since, giving then senator Barack Obama 56 percent of their vote in 2008,[38] a complete reversal of the 1984 presidential contest.

The movement of young voters away from Republicans has been even more dramatic. They split evenly for Carter and Reagan in 1980,[39] but in 1984, they went for President Reagan by a whopping 59–40 percent margin.[40] George H. W. Bush won their votes by a narrow 52–47 percent margin,[41] but this group has voted Democratic ever since then, with President Obama claiming an overwhelming 66 percent majority of their votes.[42]

Support for Republican candidates by political moderates has also been a casualty of the culture war: Reagan won their votes in both his presidential runs by substantial margins,[43] and they split evenly for George H. W. Bush in 1988.[44] But they have not voted Republican since then, and President Obama won their votes by a huge 60 to 39 percent margin over John McCain and Sarah Palin.[45]

Suburban voters have also moved into the Democratic column, going from a 61 percent majority for President Reagan in 1984[46] to a narrow 50–48 percent majority for President Obama in 2008.[47]

And finally, independents, the segment of voters who split for Ronald Reagan in 1984 by a 64–36 percent margin,[48] went for Senator Obama by a substantial 52–44 percent margin in 2008.[49] They are the swing voters who decide most elections, and it was the return of the independents to the Republican column in the 2009 and 2010 elections (based almost exclusively on economic issues) that gave Republicans such a smashing victory. But they will most likely return to the Democratic column if the Republican Party returns to its previous anti-gay agenda and other social issues rather than attend to the economic issues that most voters care about.

That all of these voter groups went from being reliably Republican to reliably Democratic, at least in presidential elections, in a span of less than twenty years, should be a wake-up call for Republicans. Unfortunately, the Religious Right's culture war has become part of the Republican "brand" over the past twenty years, and this trend has clearly turned off millions of these formerly Republican voters, many of whom no doubt have family members, relatives, friends, or colleagues who are gay. This is especially true for younger voters, whose pronounced social tolerance and preference for Democrats does not bode well for Republican candidates if they continue to espouse an anti-gay agenda.

BE CAREFUL WHAT YOU WISH FOR

It would be wise for Religious Right Republicans to realize that mixing religious beliefs with politics is a double-edged sword. Those on the left, after all, have been doing this for many years and have consequently helped build the modern welfare state we have today. The National Council for Churches (NCC), for example, has for at least fifty years promoted the modern collectivist state as the logical result of putting its Christian values of compassion and service to others into practice. To paraphrase former representative Souder, they certainly did not check their religious beliefs at the door, and our nation is the worse for it. There are, after all, many different ways to interpret what the Bible says and commands.

In addition to their missionary, evangelical, and social work, NCC member congregations have been driven by the belief that their Christian beliefs demand social and political action on their behalf, and that has included their very public support for most of the social welfare legislation passed since its founding in 1950. Surely the NCC and most modern progressives would entirely agree with the admonition of President Franklin Roosevelt that "we cannot read the history of our rise and development as a nation, without reckoning with the place the Bible has occupied in shaping the advances of the Republic. Where we have been the truest and most consistent in obeying its precepts, we have attained the greatest measure of contentment and prosperity."[50] Stirring words indeed to every theocrat, but the results of President Roosevelt's programs and policies were destructive of many of the very freedoms conservatives profess to believe in.

It's not just the historically white denominations who premise their political agenda on their religious beliefs. Many black denominations tie their Christian faith to their decidedly left-wing political agenda, perhaps best personified by both Reverends Al Sharpton and Jesse Jackson. And even further to the left have been the practitioners of the "liberation theology" movement, including the now infamous Reverend Jeremiah Wright, President Obama's minister for over twenty years in Chicago. These ministers and the millions they represent fully believe in the practice of basing government policies on "biblical principles" every bit as much as LaHaye, but to very different ends.

Even modern environmentalists have used the scriptures to build support for a variety of environmental measures, including the current push for radical global warming measures and forcibly transforming our economy to rely on different energy sources than it does now. "What Would Jesus Drive?"[51] is a question widely asked by those on the left who believe that environmentalism is not only perfectly compatible with Christian teachings but also a valid basis for enacting a variety of radical environmental measures to combat what they see as the destruction of Earth's resources.

Indeed, a coalition of left-wing groups, including the National Association for the Advancement of Colored People, the American Federation of Labor and Congress of Industrial Organizations, the Service Employees International Union, the National Council of La Raza, and a variety of environmental groups, came together for a pre-election march and rally in Washington, DC, on October 2, 2010, to promote their agenda of "jobs, justice, and education," all funded, of course, by more government spending and higher taxes.[52] Also joining in the rally were socially conservative faith groups like the National Baptist Convention and the National Missionary Baptist Convention of America, whose members clearly believe that government action on behalf of this agenda helps them to pursue their goal of a government "based on biblical principles." No doubt most at the rally agreed with the sign hoisted by one protester: "Jesus Was a Liberal."[53]

Many "progressive" religious leaders and evangelicals, in fact, sincerely believe that following in Jesus's footsteps means promoting a leftist political and economic agenda. In response to House Republicans' plan in early 2011 to cut domestic spending by at least $60 billion, a coalition of progressive Christian leaders took out a full-page ad in a Washington newspaper asking, "What Would Jesus Cut?"[54] The ad, spearheaded by Reverend Jim Wallis, head of a leftist Christian group called Sojourners, criticized the Republican cuts, arguing that cutting assistance to the poor was un-Christian and that cutting military spending was the proper thing to do. "Cutting programs that help those who need them most is morally wrong," said one supporter, highlighting the fact that there are many different ways to define and promote "morality." These same groups ran a public campaign against budget cuts during the rancorous 2011 battle over increasing the federal debt ceiling, again making the argument that social programs and spending were consistent with Christian values.[55] Certainly, in their eyes, they were also promoting a government "based on biblical principles."

Other liberal groups also see the moral hypocrisy of the Religious Right on this issue. A new group called the American Values Network began an advertising campaign in June 2011 with a video called "Christians Must Choose: Ayn Rand or Jesus."[56] It takes conservative and libertarian admirers of Ayn Rand to task[57] for promoting the anti-religion but free market philosophy of Ayn Rand, the popular novelist and writer who was adamantly opposed to both religion and the philosophy of altruism. Many Tea Party and libertarian Republicans are fans of her novels and philosophy of objectivism, including Senator Rand Paul, Representatives Paul Ryan and Ron Paul, and radio talk show host Rush Limbaugh, among many others. In fact, Ayn Rand and her trenchant political and philosophical writings were a primary reason for the emergence of the modern libertarian movement in America in the 1970s, and she remains an enduring intellectual force for much of the libertarian movement today.

The American Values Network explains, "Many who for years have been the loudest voices involving the language of faith and moral values are now praising the atheist philosopher Ayn Rand, whose teachings stand in direct contradiction to the Bible. . . . GOP leaders want to argue that they are defending Christian principles,"[58] yet they support policies and programs the group judges un-Christian. The network's website even carries statements attacking Ayn Rand and her followers from conservative evangelicals Marvin Olasky, editor of *World* magazine, and former Nixon official and convicted Watergate burglar Chuck Colson.[59] And, of course, the American Values Network has a point: what constitutes "biblical morality" is quite subjective and open to broad interpretation. The arbitrary nature of just what constitutes "defending Christian principles" is the best reason anyone can think of for keeping religion as far as possible from the halls of Congress when it comes to making public policy or spending the public's money. The words and stated beliefs of the Religious Right are now coming back to haunt the entire pro-freedom movement in this country.

But perhaps no better example exists of the danger of using government to further one's own religious beliefs than the words of then senator Barack Obama at a campaign rally on September 29, 2008. When asked by a voter about what makes him a Christian, Obama answered that "the precepts of Jesus Christ spoke to me in terms of the kind of life that I would want to lead—being my brothers' and sisters' keeper, treating others as they would treat me."[60] In fact, he told one religious gathering that with his leadership, "we can create a Kingdom right here on Earth."[61] From Presidents Roosevelt and Obama to Reverends Jim Jones and Jeremiah Wright, politicians and preachers have fought to create their very own heaven on earth by combining government activism with their own preferred moral agendas, often with disastrous results. History shows us that one casualty of this activism has been the destruction of the basic political principles that supposedly govern this nation: the sovereignty of each individual in running his or her own life.

THE GLASS HOUSE OF SOCIAL CONSERVATIVES

To those on the right who say they want a government "based on biblical principles," it's also fair to ask: Which principles, exactly, are you referring to, especially in light of the obvious double standard on the part of millions of self-professed Christians and evangelicals who insist on thrusting their faith into the public square? Clearly, many of those who believe in using government to promote their religious values are quite selective when deciding which religious values the government should promote and which it should ignore.

Even some prominent theologians in the social conservative movement have begun to acknowledge the rather obvious hypocrisy on the part of many in the Religious Right in their seeming obsession with homosexuality and gay rights. R. Albert Mohler Jr., president of the Southern Baptist Theological Seminary, recently spoke out about this issue. Writing on his website, he conceded that heterosexual "divorce harms many more lives than will be touched by homosexual marriage. . . . The real scandal is the fact that evangelical Protestants divorce at rates at least as high as the rest of the public. Needless to say, this creates a significant credibility crisis when evangelicals then rise to speak in defense of marriage."[62] Indeed. And yet we hear few calls for a constitutional amendment to ban divorce or to regulate adultery, two steps that would do far more to "protect" traditional marriage than all the anti–gay marriage amendments combined.

The severity of this hypocrisy was echoed in the spring 2010 issue of *Political Science Quarterly* in an article by University of Washington professor Mark A. Smith titled "Religion, Divorce, and the Missing Culture War in America."[63] David Gibson, religion reporter for the Politics Daily website, explained the importance of this path-breaking essay. "Even as the Religious Right organized in the 1970s and began notching political victories in the 1980s, divorce was virtually ignored while issues such as abortion, school prayer, the Equal Rights Amendment, and other hot button topics were emphasized as the real threats to society," he wrote. "This occurred even though divorce, which is clearly and strongly condemned in the Bible, was prevalent among conservative Christians. Smith's findings show that 43 percent of evangelical Protestants divorce, higher than almost any other religious group and above the national average of 39 percent. . . . Smith added that 'divorce seems to carry a more direct connection to the daily realities of families than do the bellwether culture war issues of abortion and homosexuality.'"[64] The stunning honesty, and truth, of his essay should be required reading for every anti-gay politician in the nation.

Professor Smith also pointed out that whenever the issue of heterosexual divorce arose among evangelicals, rarely did they propose legislative solutions to the problem, whereas they were all too likely to do so with regard to other moral transgressions evangelicals oppose, such as homosexuality. Rather, divorce was a problem to be addressed *within the church rather than through public policy*.[65] That, of course, was the traditional view of actions the church considered sins: work to change the hearts and minds of those who sin rather than use the power of the government to punish people or belittle their rights.

Mohler, in a stunning acknowledgment of this hypocrisy on the part of many evangelicals, writes that this double standard "is an indictment of evangelical failure and a monumental scandal of the evangelical conscience."[66] These were strong words from a leading evangelical spokesman, yet politically active organizations on the right rarely acknowledge or address them.

That failure and the scandal that Mohler acknowledges is no doubt one reason why, as David Gibson concludes, "the fight against gay marriage seems to be a losing battle in the culture wars, given that younger believers are far more gay-friendly than their parents or grandparents, and as pop icons like Christian music artist Jennifer Knapp come out of the closet. 'Ten years from now, the issue of same-sex marriage will probably no longer be on the table,' says D. Michael Lindsay, religion sociologist and author of *Faith in the Halls of Power. How Evangelicals Joined the American Elite*."[67]

In the August 2010 issue of *Christianity Today*, senior managing editor Mark Galli agreed with Mohler's premise, writing, "We cannot very well argue for the sanctity of marriage as a crucial social institution while we blithely go about divorcing and approving of remarriage at a rate that destabilizes marriage. . . . In short, we have been perfect hypocrites on this issue. Until we admit that, and take steps to amend our ways, our cries of alarm about gay marriage will echo off into oblivion."[68]

This honest discussion within the evangelical and Religious Right movements is long overdue, and it highlights the rather obvious need on the part of these movements to back off their aggressive attack on gay and lesbian rights to tend instead to their own shortcomings. Such a change of heart would certainly earn them a surge of goodwill, even from their political adversaries. It would also put an end to the moral hypocrisy described above, as well as the political hypocrisy of pursuing socially conservative policies against gays and lesbians that will destroy the very individual freedom and free enterprise these organizations and individuals say they support.

The bottom line for all conservatives and libertarians, religious or not, is this: there is simply no shortage of proposed public policies and programs instituted by the government that cannot be traced in some way to biblical teachings or phrases, yet few on the right would agree with them. In the final analysis, that is precisely the reason the wall between religion and state that Jefferson spoke of should be kept as high as possible: religious beliefs provide the justification for a whole host of actions and policies that are diametrically opposed to the basic freedoms espoused by the Founding Fathers and by most modern conservatives.

It is no exaggeration to say that one man's religion can be another man's tyranny, and the threat to our liberty comes from both the left and the right.

If Republicans want to grow as a party and attract the younger voters, women, independents, and other demographic groups it has lost in recent years, it must present a more tolerant, ecumenical face to all Americans, Christians and non-Christians alike. Embracing a socially tolerant view of gays and lesbians and welcoming them into the Republican Party rather than shunning them will go a long way toward achieving those goals.

3

WHAT ARE GAY RIGHTS?

So what do people actually mean when they talk about gay rights? Not surprisingly, there seems to be some confusion, and even a bit of intellectual dishonesty, across the political spectrum on this issue. The exact rights and issues referred to by the phrase "gay rights" have also evolved over the years since the Stonewall riot put the concept of gay rights in the middle of American culture. An issue-by-issue analysis of the major issues and legislative proposals out there today will perhaps help alleviate some of the fear and ignorance that exist in our party, especially in much of the base, about these issues. Some may be surprised at the level of Republican and conservative support for at least some gay issues.

In the early years of the gay rights movement, the primary emphasis was on the laissez-faire notion of removing the government from the regulation or prohibition of private acts between consenting adults. At the time of the 1969 Stonewall riot, every state in the union but one had a sodomy law forbidding same-sex sexual relations between consenting adults. Ending these laws became the primary focus not only of gay rights activists but also of many in the entire counterculture movement of the 1970s. "Keep your laws off my body" was not just a popular bumper sticker of the day but a real philosophy of personal freedom, as well as a political agenda.

Ending police harassment of gay businesses and their customers was another important focus of the burgeoning gay rights movement. As stated earlier, police entrapment and harassment were common occurrences, and gay activists and their supporters demanded an end to such harassment.[1] The growing political influence of the gay movement in the

1970s began to have a real effect on politics in urban areas, and gay-friendly enclaves such as San Francisco, Los Angeles, New York, and other large cities became magnets for gay people and culture.[2]

Inevitably, however, the gay rights movement took its cues, political agenda, and techniques from the black civil rights movement. Although many black leaders initially kept the gay rights movement at a distance, the civil rights movement became the model for the burgeoning gay rights movement, and both began to share a common political agenda and strategy: aggressive federal intervention on behalf of both real and imagined rights.[3]

EMPLOYMENT NONDISCRIMINATION

Perhaps at the top of the list of legislative goals was a national employment nondiscrimination law, similar to the 1964 Civil Rights Act that outlawed discrimination on the basis of race in employment and public accommodations. Five years after the Stonewall riot, in 1974, US Representatives Bella Abzug and Ed Koch (the future mayor of New York City) introduced the Gay Rights Bill, H.R. 14752.[4] It sought to add "sexual orientation" to the other categories covered by the Civil Rights Act of 1964, but it didn't gain much traction.

In 1994, gay rights advocates in Congress introduced the Employment Non-Discrimination Act (ENDA),[5] which has been introduced in every Congress since then save for one. It focuses solely on employment discrimination based on sexual orientation in the private sector. It has failed every time, most often due to lack of support or outright hostility from Republicans, although some Republicans over the years have supported the bill or even co-sponsored it, such as Representatives Chris Shays from Connecticut and Ileana Ros-Lehtinen from Florida. The last time it was voted on in the House, in 2007 (only once, even though the Democrats controlled Congress up through the 2010 elections), it received the support of thirty-five Republican House members.[6] Although it failed by just one vote in the Senate in 1996, it has never come to another vote there.

Ironically, however, during the past decade or so, the very same bill has been losing support on the left because it does not include what is called "gender identity and expression." That phrase refers to "transgender" men and women—that is, those who feel they were born into the wrong sex and therefore identify as a member of the opposite sex. Some choose to undergo sex-change operations to become the sex they believe they were intended to be.

To millions of Americans, supporters and opponents of gay rights alike, the subject of transgender individuals is an uncomfortable one to discuss, but many supporters of gay rights have expanded their mission to include self-identified transgender people.[7] They now demand that proposed laws like ENDA include gender identity and expression along with the more traditional category of sexual orientation. This has caused a sometimes bitter split in the broader gay rights movement between those who believe that outlawing discrimination on the basis of sexual orientation should be the primary purpose of gay activism (as it has been for nearly forty years) and those who not only demand that various legislative proposals include gender identity and expression but also actively oppose any legislation that does not, even if such opposition spells defeat for the bill.[8]

This demand to include gender identity simply makes the passage of an employment nondiscrimination bill (and other legislation) much more difficult and in many cases, at the state and local level, nearly impossible. Currently, just fifteen states and the District of Columbia have nondiscrimination policies that include both sexual orientation and gender identity, while nine states have policies that protect sexual orientation only.[9]

Polls show that most Americans support employment nondiscrimination policies that include sexual orientation, for both the public and private sectors. Both Gallup and *Newsweek* have been polling on this question for more than thirty years, and the results are quite clear. By overwhelming majorities, Americans support a policy of employment nondiscrimination for gays and lesbians.[10] Since 1986, Gallup has shown more than 80 percent in support of this policy, with its May 2008 poll showing 87 percent favoring such a policy.[11] *Newsweek*'s December 2008 poll showed 87 percent in support.[12] Contrary to popular opinion, this includes all parts of the political spectrum, including Republicans and even social conservatives.[13]

As far back as 1996, a poll by Greenberg Research showed that among Christians generally, 70 percent believed gays and lesbians should be protected from job discrimination.[14] That same poll showed that even among fundamentalist and evangelical Christians, support for such protection was at 60 percent.[15] A Tarrance Group poll in 1997 showed 59 percent of Republicans in support of ENDA,[16] and a 2007 poll by Republican pollster Tony Fabrizio showed an overwhelming 77 percent of Republicans supporting protection from job discrimination based on sexual orientation.[17]

Yet, despite this overwhelming rank-and-file Republican support, most GOP members of Congress and state legislatures oppose employment nondiscrimination legislation, in most cases simply because of the disproportionately loud opposition from Religious Right organizations. Like most elected officials, Republican officeholders respond to those who raise their voices the loudest, but by doing so, they have helped paint a picture of the party as out of touch not only with Republican voters but also with Americans at large. That is not smart politics, to say the least. As stated earlier, millions of moderate and independent voters have drifted away from the Republican Party as it has become more closely identified with the vocal Religious Right.

The Republican Party's growing libertarian wing, however, makes the issue of nondiscrimination bills more complex than it may first appear. That's because most libertarians, and even some conservatives, begin the discussion of nondiscrimination laws by making the all-important distinction between the public and private sectors. The larger issue for them regarding private-sector discrimination is whether they should support a proposed bill like ENDA at all, given how it would further regulate private-sector transactions and employment decisions. Several different considerations about this issue therefore require some thoughtful attention by all Republicans.

Libertarians clearly have a general philosophical objection to the government telling private businesses the basis on which they must hire and fire their employees, so it's easy to understand their objection to expanding such laws to include new categories. And, in fact, private business is generally already far ahead of government in eliminating employment discrimination on the basis of sexual orientation.

According to the Employee Benefits Research Institute, not only do most Fortune 500 companies have policies in place prohibiting such discrimination but they also extend domestic partner benefits such as health insurance to their employees.[18] In fact, the number of companies that receive the Human Rights Campaign's (a national gay and lesbian rights organization) top corporate ratings jumped from just 12 in 2002 to 337 in 2011.[19] Given the dramatic changes in business employment practices regarding gay and lesbian employees that have already taken place in corporate America, passage of ENDA might be a mostly symbolic act rather than one that brings substantive changes to America's workplaces. Even so, the exclusion of gays and lesbians from federal employment nondiscrimination laws does raise the issue of equal protection under the law, or lack thereof, and that should also be a consideration for libertarians and conservatives.

Social conservative leaders and their Republican representatives in Congress, after all, oppose inclusion of gays and lesbians under nondiscrimination laws based simply on their own personal anti-gay religious beliefs, not on any kind of principled opposition to government coercion in the private sector. Many conservative leaders have stated quite explicitly that they don't object to antidiscrimination laws when they cover racial minorities, religious minorities, women, veterans, and the other categories included in most antidiscrimination statutes.[20] In principle, such laws are fine; it's only when they cover gays, lesbians, and transgender people that they raise objections.

Considering the Right's clearly stated double standard, its standard complaint that such laws create "special rights" for gays and lesbians is obviously bogus. One can only conclude that the opposition to such laws by some conservatives is therefore based mostly on personal animus toward homosexuals. In a free country, of course, people have the right to hold such views, but they should not be the basis for public policy that governs all of us, including gays and lesbians.

Perhaps the only principled libertarian position on such laws is either to cover all such groups that have suffered from discrimination historically, including gays and lesbians, or to abolish such laws altogether (or at least to call for such abolition). To have such laws on the books but intentionally not include the gay and lesbian community is really to throw the principle of equal protection under the law out the window. A fundamental principle of a libertarian government, after all, is to treat all citizens the same legally, not to have the state grant special treatment or legal privileges to favored groups and to withhold them from others. That is what the phrase "equal protection of the laws" means, and excluding gay and lesbian Americans from such laws would clearly seem to violate that principle.

It's not hard to understand, of course, the fear that deeply religious people have about the rapid changes taking place in American culture, which has clearly become saturated with references to sexuality, including sexual orientation, not to mention the increasing visibility of transgender people, a phenomenon that is simply inexplicable to millions of (perhaps most) Americans. But social conservatives will never get others to sympathize with their fears or respect their desire to insulate themselves from the people or cultural influences they dislike (to the limited extent possible in a free society) until they learn to give others the same kind of respect for autonomy and control over their lives. Freedom of association and respect for it is a two-way street, but such tolerance has been lacking on the right for some time. After all, much of the political agenda of the Religious Right has for years been focused on conservative social engineering using government power—from outlawing private sexual relations to prohibiting any form of legal recognition of same-sex couples, to forbidding equal access to government programs and opportunities by gay and lesbian Americans.[21] The Religious Right has waged an all-out assault on the principle of equality under the law for gays and lesbians for forty years, and that assault must stop if this country is to live up to its ideal (the Republican ideal) of maximizing individual liberty and expression.

The fault does not lie solely with the Religious Right, of course. Many secularists have also used state power to force others to accept their personal values, including tolerance of homosexuality and other personal characteristics some religious people object to. The difference, however, is that the Left has never premised its entire political agenda on a general belief in individual liberty, free enterprise, and limited government. The Right has, and so we have every right to demand that those on the right be consistent in promoting a pro-freedom agenda. So far, they have fallen quite short of this expectation. It's no wonder, therefore, that the Right is widely perceived by millions of Americans and many Republicans to be against, rather than for, the ideas of personal freedom and individual rights. That widely held perception is certainly detrimental to the Republican Party.

PUBLIC-SECTOR DISCRIMINATION

ENDA is not the only federal gay rights issue that Republicans need to address. There is also the related issue of public-sector discrimination, not just in federal employment but also in government benefits and privileges. These issues genuinely go to the heart of the principle of equal protection under the law. There is none of the moral ambiguity that may exist in the discussion about private-sector discrimination. For libertarians at least, the principle of equality under the law should be crystal clear when it comes to the government and the way it treats its employees and citizens.

Unfortunately, there is currently no law regarding federal employment discrimination against gays and lesbians. Federal employees have been covered since 1998 by an executive order issued by President Bill Clinton, the first time federal employees were protected from job discrimination on the basis of sexual orientation. Amazingly, some Republicans objected to it at the time, but one of President George W. Bush's first acts when he took office was to renew Clinton's executive order for his own administration,[22] although he came under fire from Religious Right leaders for doing so, another indicator of the huge disconnect between the American people and the self-appointed guardians of America's morality.

Ideally, there should be a simple statute that forbids employment discrimination on the basis of sexual orientation in the federal workforce. At the very least, a Republican candidate for president should pledge to renew this executive order if elected. Republicans at the state and local levels as well should support policies that forbid employment discrimination on the basis of sexual orientation by government agencies.

A related issue to federal employment protection is the bill first proposed in 2007 called the Domestic Partnership Benefits and Obligations Act that would have equalized some of the benefits federal employees receive, benefits such as health insurance and retirement savings.[23] These benefits currently go only to spouses, which, of course, discriminates against all unmarried couples, gay and straight. Employees who are denied such benefits therefore actually receive a much lower salary for the same work. In reality, giving such benefits only to married employees constitutes providing "special rights" for them, which is fundamentally unfair and discriminatory.

The Domestic Partnership Benefits and Obligations Act would correct this imbalance by providing the same family benefits to lesbian and gay employees (and unmarried straight couples) that married employees already receive, such as health insurance, life insurance, and other benefits routinely included in policies covering employees with spouses. To receive these benefits, the employees would have to submit an affidavit of eligibility with the Office of Personnel Management certifying that the employee and his or her partner meet the necessary criteria. Unmarried straight and gay employees, of course, perform the same work and pay the same taxes as married employees, so clearly the current two-tiered system of compensation is wrong and violates the principle of equal pay for equal work, not to mention equal protection under the law.

Not only is basing opposition to this bill on personal religious values and beliefs mean-spirited, it also clearly violates the concepts of basic fairness and equal access to government services and employment that our party historically stood for. Simple justice should dictate that all taxpayers and federal employees receive equal access to government benefits. The denial of such benefits to some helps deprive the federal government of good workers who will go instead to private industry, which is often much friendlier in its workplace policies.

The argument that the federal government can't really afford such benefits is really just a ruse that overlooks this obvious point: if these benefits were to go instead to spouses of heterosexual employees, no one would question the cost. It is only because they would go to same-sex partners that opponents raise a fiscal argument against them. Obviously, it's not the relatively small amount of money (between $600 and $900 million a year out of $200 billion a year in salaries and benefits for federal employees)[24] but the would-be *recipients* of the money that concerns such critics. It's nothing more than yet another way to punish people they don't like. Gays and lesbians make up about 5 percent of the federal workforce, however, and they should receive the same benefits as a matter of simple fairness.[25]

When first introduced in the 111th session of Congress, the bill drew a number of Republican co-sponsors, including Senators Susan Collins of Maine and Gordon Smith of Oregon and Representatives Ileana Ros-Lehtinen of Florida, Chris Shays of Connecticut, and Tom Davis of Virginia. Even during that Democrat-controlled Congress, however, the bill never came up for votes in the full Senate or House. It was introduced again in November 2011, but as of this writing, Representative Ros-Lehtinen was the sole Republican sponsor in the House, and Senator Collins was the only Republican sponsor in the Senate. A vote in either chamber is unlikely in 2012. The merits of such a bill will remain, however, and it will continue to be a centerpiece in the fight for equality at the federal level.

A majority of Americans apparently agree with the aims of this bill. A Quinnipiac University poll from July 2011 asked voters if the law prohibiting federal benefits for same-sex spouses should be repealed or retained. A substantial majority of 59 percent opposed this law, up from 54 percent in 2009.[26] A *Newsweek* poll from 2008 showed large majorities in favor of a variety of health insurance, Social Security, and other employee benefits for gay and lesbian domestic partners (73, 67, and 73 percent, respectively).[27] Such majorities obviously include very substantial numbers of Republicans.

A somewhat related bill, the Tax Equity for Health Plan Beneficiaries Act, was introduced in the 2011 session of Congress, also with bipartisan support.[28] This bill would allow partners of unmarried employees in the private sector to deduct the cost of their health insurance from their taxable income, just as married couples are allowed to do. Currently, such partner coverage is considered taxable income for all unmarried employees. Because of this policy, employers collectively pay $57 million per year in additional payroll taxes, while unmarried employees with partner benefits pay, on average, $1,069 in additional income taxes each year.[29] Given their desire to maximize private health insurance coverage and minimize the tax burden on average citizens, Republicans should find this bill completely compatible with their stated beliefs. Their support for such a measure, however, remains to be seen. Given the large majorities of adults in favor of other nondiscrimination measures protecting gay and lesbian Americans, one would be hard pressed to argue that substantial public opposition to federal tax equity for them exists.

HATE CRIME LEGISLATION

Even with a Democratic president and overwhelming Democratic control of Congress, the only pro–gay rights bill other than the repeal of Don't Ask, Don't Tell (DADT) signed into law during Barack Obama's administration has been the Matthew Shepard and James Byrd, Jr., Hate Crimes Prevention Act of 2009, which was actually tacked onto the defense spending bill, a tactic that drew much criticism from Republicans. The bill, named after two murdered victims of hate crimes, added sexual orientation and gender identity to the existing federal hate crime statute. Ironically, the perpetrators in these two murder cases were prosecuted to the fullest extent of the law, leaving one to wonder why these two victims were chosen as symbols of the alleged need for increased federal hate crime protection.

While many conservatives and libertarians made principled arguments against the bill based on the inclusion of enhanced penalties for perpetrators of hate crimes and federal intervention into local law enforcement, the Religious Right veered off into outrageous claims about "special rights for homosexuals" and characterized the bill as an attack on freedom of religion. These are the same folks who do not oppose the statute when it's applied to other minorities but are outraged that gay and lesbian victims of hate crimes are now included.

The law has nothing to do with freedom of speech or religion, as claimed by some on the right: it targets violent crime, not speech. Contrary to these dishonest claims, ministers can—and do—say whatever they want in their pulpits about their religious beliefs and their views on homosexuality without fear of retaliation. In fact, no hate crime statute in this country has ever been used to silence the clergy or anyone else. The federal law, like all hate crime legislation, targets someone only after an actual crime has been committed: that's when its provisions come into play.

It is quite true that the prevalence of hate crimes is sometimes vastly overstated by some on the left.[30] Such crimes, in fact, constitute an extremely low percentage of all violent crime. In 2001, for example, of the 13,752 total homicides reported by the FBI, only 10 were classified as hate crimes, and just one of those involved a gay person. More recent FBI statistics from 2010 show the same low number of violent hate crimes, including murder.[31] Both sides in this debate have in fact made wildly inaccurate claims about hate crimes. Any federal law on this issue will be mostly symbolic since most hate crimes do not even involve the use of physical force.

Conservatives and libertarians are clearly right to oppose what are called enhanced penalties—that is, additional penalties when a crime is motivated by racial, anti-gay, or other forms of personal bias. The 2009 statute, for example, added ten years of prison time automatically to a crime of violence in which anti-gay bias played a part. Even some civil libertarians on the left oppose this two-tiered system of punishment in which similar crimes result in different punishments, depending on the beliefs and motives of the perpetrators.

Yet many of the conservative critics of this law have never spoken out against hate crime laws and disparate penalties when applied to people other than gays and lesbians. Where were their concerns for free speech and different standards of justice then? Even seemingly level-headed people like Representative Mike Pence are led to make silly and hypocritical statements, like this one after the passage of the federal hate crime act: "I resent this measure [because] we're now adding resources and money to investigate and prosecute crimes against certain people [gays and lesbians] that aren't available for the same crime committed against others. Any violence is heinous and justice should remain blind." Indeed, it should, but Representative Pence and virtually every other Republican leader who has spoken out about this bill never publicly objected to federal hate crime statutes until gays and lesbians were added. They're apparently not troubled at all by including race, religion, ethnicity, national origin, and the numerous other protected categories.

That kind of hypocrisy and false outrage rightfully earns the scorn of many and makes a laughing stock of the Republican Party. No wonder many people see nothing but a rather transparent case of homophobia in the case of Representative Pence and other opponents. Fortunately, Pence's hypocrisy is shared by a rapidly shrinking percentage of the American people, and Republican politicians must wake up to the fact that parroting such views will lose the votes of the very swing voters they need to win elections.

In fact, according to FBI figures, homosexuals are 2.4 times more likely to be the victim of a hate crime attack than Jews,[32] 2.6 times more likely than blacks,[33] 4.4 times more likely than Muslims,[34] and 13.8 times more likely than Latinos.[35] If we're going to have a federal hate crime statute, there can be no justification for not including gay and lesbian Americans under its protection.

Now that the federal statute includes gays and lesbians, it's no more likely that it will be repealed than it was prior to the addition of this group to the other protected classes. Republicans can attempt to reduce or, better yet, eliminate the enhanced penalties feature of the law, and that would be a legitimate goal based on sound libertarian principles like equal protection under the law. But they need to reject the dishonest arguments made by some conservatives that adding sexual orientation to the existing federal statute will somehow erode freedom of speech and religion. That charge is utterly without a rational foundation.

DON'T ASK, DON'T TELL

Another contentious federal issue within the Republican Party has been the seventeen-year-old Don't Ask, Don't Tell law, which prohibited gays and lesbians from serving openly in the armed forces. Although DADT was finally repealed in the December 2010 lame-duck session of Congress, it's important to examine the issues involved because many on the right still oppose repeal of the policy, some based on mistaken beliefs rather than simple hatred of homosexuals, although the latter is clearly prevalent in many anti-gay organizations. A majority of the Republican presidential contenders have even called for a reinstatement of DADT.

DADT was actually a compromise initiated in 1993 by President Clinton that allowed gays and lesbians to serve in the military, but only if they essentially remained in the closet. Telling fellow soldiers or officers about their sexual orientation violated the "don't tell" part of the equation. President Clinton had initially proposed allowing gays to serve openly, but after a firestorm of criticism from Republicans and even some Democrats, Clinton agreed to DADT as a middle path. Retired senator Barry Goldwater, however, argued for full repeal of the prohibition on gay soldiers by pointing out, "You don't have to be straight to shoot straight."[36]

Prior to DADT, gays and lesbians were forbidden from serving at all, although many did. In 2007, it was estimated that about sixty-five thousand gays and lesbians were serving in all branches of the armed services.[37] Since DADT was implemented, almost 13,500 have been discharged for violation of the policy,[38] even during the wars in Iraq and Afghanistan. The cost of replacing those thousands expelled has been enormous. According to a recent Pentagon audit, the cost of replacing the 3,660 gay troops kicked out of the military from 2004 until 2009 was $193 million.[39] Nearly 40 percent of those discharged, in fact, held infantry or security roles or had critical foreign-language skills desperately needed over the past few years with two wars being fought in the Middle East.[40]

Proponents of keeping DADT warn of the threat to unit cohesion and morale posed by allowing openly gay people to serve. Yet the same charge was made back when the armed services were racially integrated by President Harry Truman. Many southern soldiers were very opposed to serving with blacks, but President Truman understood that personal discomfort with, or even hatred of, African Americans by some white soldiers was not a legitimate reason to bar them from serving in the regular units, no matter how much it broke with military tradition.

In fact, most polls have shown an increasing willingness on the part of enlisted members to allow gays to serve openly. In 2006, long before repeal of DADT was seriously on Congress's radar screen, a Zogby poll of military members found that 27 percent favored allowing gays to serve, while 37 percent were unsure or had no preference;[41] 37 percent were opposed.[42] Fully 73 percent of the respondents said they felt comfortable in the presence of gay and lesbian personnel,[43] and 64 percent said homosexuals serving openly would have no impact on their unit's morale.[44] Even an article in a 2009 issue of *Joint Force Quarterly* by the Air Force's Colonel Om Prakash argued that there was no scientific evidence that repealing DADT would hurt morale.

Since then, support among enlisted men and women for serving alongside gay and lesbian service members has continued to grow. During the 2010 debate in Congress over whether to repeal DADT, the Pentagon commissioned a study of men and women serving in the armed forces to determine how they felt about possible repeal of the policy. As part of that study, a detailed questionnaire was sent to over four hundred thousand service members asking for their opinion on the issue.[45] The full report, published in December 2010, showed that more than 70 percent of the respondents thought the effects of ending DADT would be "positive, mixed, or nonexistent."[46] While 58 percent of marines in combat units said they felt homosexuals openly serving in their unit would negatively affect it, 84 percent of those who had previously served with an openly gay marine said that there would be no effect or that the effect would be positive.[47] Clearly, whatever apprehension soldiers or marines initially feel about serving with openly gay colleagues largely disappears after they have actually served with them.

Despite implementation problems that will no doubt be encountered in the process of ending the ban, most of the military leadership, including then secretary of defense Robert Gates and then chairman of the Joint Chiefs of Staff Mike Mullen, supported repeal of this policy. The only service chief who flatly opposed ending the ban, in fact, was Marine Corps commandant General James Amos. Other officers who have stated their support for ending the ban include James E. Cartwright, vice chairman of the Joint Chiefs of Staff; commander of the US Army Europe, General Carter F. Ham; Admiral Gary Roughhead, chief of naval operations; General Norton A. Schwartz, Air Force chief of staff; and former chairman of the Joint Chiefs of Staff and former secretary of state Colin Powell. One can hardly imagine they all support repeal merely out of a desire to be politically correct, a charge leveled by some supporters of DADT against those who came out for repeal.

Even Commandant Amos issued a statement addressed to his troops following the repeal of DADT, telling them they would be expected to faithfully and fully follow all orders regarding implementation of the new policy. "As we implement repeal, I want leaders at all levels to reemphasize the importance of maintaining dignity and respect for one another. . . . We are Marines, we care for one another and respect the rights of all who wear this uniform,"[48] he said, winning the praise of many who had been on the other side of the repeal debate.

The experience of our major allies with gay service members also shows that the reservations of some about changing the policy are unfounded. In fact, of the twenty-six US allies that participate in NATO, fully twenty-two permit gays to serve openly.[49] All European Union countries except Greece do the same. Britain, France, the Netherlands, Germany, Canada, New Zealand, Portugal, Australia, Italy, and Israel, among others, are bewildered by America's archaic policy, and even hard-core bigots would be hard pressed to explain how the military readiness and effectiveness of these major allies, particularly our allies in Iraq and Afghanistan, have been harmed by their policy of allowing gays to serve.

Despite all the dire predictions by right-wing groups about the negative consequences of permitting openly gay service members into our armed forces, including an anticipated mass exodus of straight service members that never happened (and never will), the end of Don't Ask, Don't Tell was certified on July 28, 2011, allowing openly gay individuals to serve beginning on September 26, 2011.[50] The United States now joins virtually all its military allies in permitting gays and lesbians to serve openly.

On this issue as well, the federal government and the Republican leadership in Congress have lagged far behind the American people. For many years, a large majority of Americans, including rank-and-file Republicans, have consistently supported ending DADT and allowing gays to serve openly. In a 2008 *Washington Post*/ABC News poll, 75 percent of Americans, including 66 percent of conservatives and 75 percent of independents, supported allowing openly gay people to serve.[51] A February 2010 Quinnipiac University poll showed 57 percent in support.[52] A CBS News/*New York Times* poll from the same period showed 58 percent favoring gays serving openly and just 28 percent opposed.[53] Gallup and *Newsweek* have been polling this question for many years, and since 1996, support for allowing gays to serve has never been below 65 percent.[54] A Gallup poll from December 2010 showed 68 percent of voters, including 51 percent of conservatives, in support of repeal.[55] Just 28 percent of voters were opposed.[56]

Many prominent conservatives have supported ending DADT, including Dick Cheney, Donald Rumsfeld, newly elected Republican senator Pat Toomey of Pennsylvania, *Weekly Standard* columnist Stephen Hayes, former New York City mayor Rudy Giuliani, *American Spectator* columnist Philip Klein, Fox News analyst Margaret Hoover, and longtime Cheney advisor Mary Matalin, among others. Support for repeal has become a thoroughly mainstream conservative position.

The huge disconnect on DADT between rank-and-file Republicans and conservatives and those in Congress and among the GOP leadership was apparent in the congressional voting on whether to repeal the policy. Despite solid support for ending DADT among Republican voters, only five Republicans in the House (including libertarian representative Ron Paul) in its first 2010 vote supported repeal; in its second vote in December, that number rose to just fifteen, including some well-known conservatives like Representatives David Drier, Mary Bono Mack, Jeff Flake, and John Campbell. The overwhelming majority of Republicans voted to keep DADT.

The same was true in the Senate, but in the final Senate vote on the repeal bill in December 2010, eight Republicans voted with all of the Democrats and two independents, producing a solid 65–31 majority in favor of repeal.[57] Those eight included conservatives John Ensign (NV), Richard Burr (NC), Mark Kirk (IL), and Scott Brown (MA). They were joined by Senators Lisa Murkowski (AK), George Voinovich (OH), Olympia Snowe (ME), and Susan Collins (ME).[58] While not all Republicans voting against repeal were motivated by anti-gay animus, this general opposition by elected Republicans is yet another example of our party's agenda being driven by a minority of activists far out of the mainstream of both America and the Republican Party. For the sake of our party, Republicans must make clear their support for this historic change and repudiate calls to bring back DADT by Far Right organizations and some of the Republican presidential candidates, such as Tim Pawlenty, Rick Santorum, Rick Perry, Newt Gingrich, and Michele Bachmann. The party of Lincoln should be leading the fight for equality before the law, not standing in its way.

One Republican organization, the national pro–gay rights group Log Cabin Republicans, led the way on this issue, first filing a suit in 2004 challenging the constitutionality of the DADT policy. After a six-year court battle, the suit resulted in a US district court ruling on September 9, 2010, that the DADT law was unconstitutional,[59] providing a big boost for those fighting for legislative repeal. The court stated that DADT violated service members' rights to free speech and due process. The presiding judge in that case, Virginia A. Phillips, consequently issued an injunction against the federal government's enforcement of the DADT policy.

Ironically, the Obama administration, despite its vow to overturn the law, requested that Judge Phillips refrain from enforcing the injunction because the repeal bill was before Congress, and the Pentagon review and survey of service members was still under way. With legislative repeal now a reality and certified by President Obama, however, the case has come to a successful conclusion, and our fully integrated American armed forces can turn their full attention to protecting this country.

SODOMY LAWS

Laws that prohibited voluntary sexual relations between consenting adults were declared unconstitutional by the Supreme Court in the 2003 *Lawrence v. Texas* case, when thirteen states still had such laws on the books, nine of them explicitly targeting homosexual relations. As the Cato Institute's amicus brief in this case stated, "The Declaration of Independence announced that 'all men are created equal.' Applying this principle to the states, the Framers of the 14th Amendment emphasized that 'the American system rests on the assertion of the equal right of every man to life, liberty, and the pursuit of happiness.'"[60] Writing for the 6–3 majority, Justice Anthony Kennedy delivered an opinion that could have been penned by any libertarian, declaring that the "Texas statute furthers no legitimate state interest which can justify its intrusion into the personal and private life of the individual."[61] Such intervention violates the presumption of liberty that runs throughout the Constitution. On the other hand, some conservatives, such as Justice Clarence Thomas, responded that sodomy laws may be silly, but the Constitution still did not prohibit the states from enforcing them. If they were to be repealed, he said, it should happen at the state level.

These opposing arguments encapsulate the division on the right about the issue of "judicial activism": the libertarian belief in the right of judges to strike down unjust laws that violate individual freedom versus the conservative notion of nearly unlimited majoritarianism, whereby individual rights are often subject to the approval of legislative or popular majorities, in many cases negating the concept of fundamental natural rights common to all men. Some Far Right religious organizations were up in arms over the case, fearing that a loss in this case would affect future court cases affecting broader issues of gay rights. Alan Sears from the Alliance Defense Fund, for example, denigrated some of the justices on the Court, saying they had "acted like they were unaware of the most basic legal precepts [such as the right] to regulate the 'health, safety and morals' of their citizens,"[62] including placing "limits on their sexual behavior,"[63] such as, for instance, on pedophilia and incest. The idea that there may—and should—be limits on state power over private conduct never occurred to Sears and his accomplices. And it still does not to this day. Fortunately, the Supreme Court in this case at least took the spirit of the Fourteenth Amendment to heart and struck down all the remaining state sodomy laws.

Fortunately, the libertarian notion of principled judicial activism is gaining new adherents on the right because the fundamental issues involved touch every area of human liberty, from economic to personal freedom. The same philosophical principles of liberty that provide the framework for free markets and limited government apply as well to personal freedom.

Voters clearly support consigning sodomy laws to the dustbin of history. Gallup has polled the public for more than thirty years on whether there should be laws against homosexual relations between consenting adults, and majorities consistently oppose such laws.[64] In May 2003, for example, 60 percent of Americans thought there should be no laws outlawing private homosexual acts according to a Gallup poll.[65] Once the *Lawrence v. Texas* opinion was released later that year, a Harris Interactive poll showed that 74 percent of Americans favored the Court's decision.[66] Darin Johnson, vice president of the communications firm that commissioned the poll, said, "It is clear that an overwhelming majority of Americans believe the Supreme Court should overturn all state laws that interfere with private sexual relations between consenting adults, whether same-sex or opposite-sex couples."[67] It seemed the country had seen the end of these intrusive laws, especially with the stamp of approval from the US Supreme Court.

Unfortunately, that is not the case. Some Religious Right organizations, such as the Family Research Council, still bang the drums for actually reinstating state sodomy laws,[68] even in the face of the *Lawrence v. Texas* decision, and some of the thirteen states that had sodomy laws on the books at the time of the Court's decision still have not repealed them. Perhaps no other issue better symbolizes contempt for the autonomy of free individuals on the part of some conservatives than this continued opposition to this fundamental human right.

Although typically not enforced, these laws are sometimes used to harass or intimidate citizens who have done no wrong, as was the case in Texas when two men were cited under the "homosexual conduct" law in the state's penal code for kissing in public. Although the men were not charged, some in the state legislature are not only stonewalling a repeal of the statute but also seeking to effectively reinstate it, and Texas governor Rick Perry has expressed support for such a measure.[69] Even in conservative Texas, a strong majority of citizens support some form of legal recognition for gay couples (63 percent in a 2010 *Texas Tribune* poll),[70] and yet some in the legislature still won't accept the Court's decision.

Republicans in Texas and around the country would be wise not just to steer clear of this issue but also to reaffirm the fundamental libertarian belief in freedom by explicitly opposing sodomy laws and wiping them off the legislative books.

DEFENSE OF MARRIAGE ACT

Congress passed the federal Defense of Marriage Act (DOMA) with just one dissenting Republican vote in 1996, and it was signed into law by President Bill Clinton. Introduced by then Republican representative Bob Barr of Georgia, the bill was a response to a court decision in Hawaii declaring that state's law against same-sex unions unconstitutional, generating uproar in Congress, particularly by those leading the charge against gay and lesbian rights.

DOMA said that no state or other jurisdiction needed to recognize any same-sex marriage concluded or recognized in another state. More importantly, it also said the federal government could not recognize same-sex marriages from any state for any federal purpose, such as, for example, offering health insurance and other benefits to partners of unmarried federal employees or allowing same-sex couples to file joint tax returns. In 2004, the Government Accounting Office issued a report containing a list of 1,138 specific federal laws that list marital status as a criterion for eligibility for benefits, protections, and responsibilities that DOMA denies to same-sex couples. This list includes the following:

- Social Security spousal protections that enhance a family's economic security while living in old age or upon disability or death
- Protections that enable one spouse to stay in the family home when the other spouse needs Medicaid for nursing home care
- The ability to have a family policy of health insurance and also to receive family health insurance from an employer without an added tax burden that applies to the cost of coverage for unmarried families
- Joint tax filing and deductions for married couples that can save families money
- Family medical leave from a job to care for a seriously ill spouse
- Disability, dependency, or death benefits for the spouses of veterans and public safety officers
- Employment benefits for federal employees, including access to family health benefits, as well as retirement and death benefits for spouses
- Estate/death protections that allow a spouse to leave assets to the other spouse—including the family home—without incurring a tax penalty
- The ability to sponsor a nonresident spouse for purposes of immigration[71]

DOMA has imposed large financial burdens on same-sex couples. A study released in late 2011 by CNN and H&R Block, for example, showed that such couples are paying up to $6,000 more in federal taxes because they are not allowed to file joint tax returns as married heterosexual couples are.[72] Filing jointly allows couples to combine their income and deductions, allowing for substantially lower tax bills.

When DOMA was first passed, of course, no states had legal same-sex marriage, and perhaps its supporters thought that DOMA would help ensure that none ever would. But now that six states do—and more will in the near future—the act is clearly usurping the rights of the states to determine their own marriage laws and punishing them for daring to be different.

DOMA is particularly controversial because it goes beyond the powers granted to Congress by the Full Faith and Credit Clause of the Constitution that compels the individual states to recognize laws and contracts passed in other states, including marriage laws. On this basis, many constitutional experts considered DOMA unconstitutional from its inception. Other court challenges against DOMA have risen as well, particularly in recent years.

In November 2010, for example, the American Civil Liberties Union filed a suit on behalf of Edie Windsor, an eighty-year-old lesbian in New York.[73] Edie and her partner, Thea Spyer, were an elderly, legally married lesbian couple. Their forty-four-year partnership far outstripped in longevity millions of heterosexual marriages. They were married in Canada in 2003 but lived in New York, where their marriage was legally recognized. But when Thea died in 2009, the IRS stuck Edie with a $350,000 estate tax bill,[74] an amount she would not owe if she had married a man instead of a woman. Their emotional story has touched many people and was made into a movie titled *Edie and Thea: A Very Long Engagement.* Like the other eighty thousand legally married same-sex couples in the United States, Edie and Thea suffered real economic hardship due to the clearly discriminatory consequences of DOMA.

In Connecticut, a group called Gay & Lesbian Advocates & Defenders (GLAD) filed a suit in *Pedersen v. Office of Personnel Management* on behalf of a group of former federal employees.[75] The case is summarized on GLAD's website: "This lawsuit challenges the federal government's denial of marriage-related protections in the areas of federal Family Medical Leave Act benefits, federal laws for private pension plans, federal laws concerning state pension plans, as well as the same core issues addressed in GLAD's case of *Gill v. OPM*—federal income taxation social security benefits, and employment benefits for federal employees and retirees."[76]

Until February 23, 2011, there had been few other challenges to the law other than the two court cases cited above. On that day, however, the Obama administration announced a reversal of its previous policy of defending DOMA against lawsuits challenging its constitutionality. The Justice Department will accordingly take the new position that the law should be struck down as a violation of the Equal Protection Clause of the Constitution, even though the administration says it will continue to enforce the law, a somewhat confusing, though legal, distinction. The Obama administration now argues that because DOMA explicitly denies equal protection to a specific group of citizens, it is presumed to be unconstitutional unless there is a compelling governmental interest in enacting that unequal protection.[77]

Unfortunately, in response to this policy change by the administration, the House Republican leadership, in the form of the so-called Bipartisan Legal Advisory Group (BLAG), stepped in to challenge this new policy by arguing in court filings that DOMA is constitutional and that Congress has the authority to arbitrarily decide what the definition of marriage is regardless of what the states decide, thereby overturning the right of the states to determine their own marriage policies. It is unfortunate that the Obama administration is exhibiting greater support for federalism and the Tenth Amendment than the Republican Congress.

After all, it is not simply liberals who consider the law unconstitutional. Charles Fried, who served as solicitor general in the Ronald Reagan administration and is now a law professor at Harvard, also believes that DOMA is unconstitutional,[78] although he finds the administration's dual positions of enforcing the law while also refusing to defend it in court "incoherent." Former Republican representative Bob Barr, who wrote and introduced the law, has changed his views on it; he now considers it unconstitutional and a gross violation of the Tenth Amendment and the general principle of federalism that supposedly animates the conservative movement in this country.[79]

Even Pat Vaughn, the attorney for the American Family Association, one of the most extreme social conservative, anti-gay groups in the nation, made the following statement shortly after the Obama administration announced its change of heart: "The Defense of Marriage Act is probably unconstitutional, particularly if you attempt to apply it to say that a marriage conducted in one state is not in effect in another. That clearly violates the Constitution."[80] Clearly, at least in this case, Vaughn's intellectual honesty trumped his usual opposition to gay rights. The fact that so many social conservative organizations and activists support DOMA simply tells us that hypocrisy runs rampant on the right, not that there is some intellectually honest conservative argument that justifies it, especially in light of the Right's claim of fidelity to the principle of federalism.

Contrary to the usual bloviating from some on the right about how the public "overwhelmingly" opposes same-sex marriage, a slim majority of Americans now oppose the Defense of Marriage Act. According to an August 2010 poll by the Associated Press and the National Constitution Center, 52 percent of Americans believe the federal government should recognize same-sex marriages, while 46 percent said it should not.[81] These figures closely mirror the polling data on same-sex marriage itself.

A March 2011 poll conducted by the Human Rights Campaign in partnership with the polling firm Greenberg Quinlan Rosner Research showed 51 percent of registered voters oppose DOMA, while just 34 percent favor it.[82] Independent voters, so important to future Republican electoral prospects, oppose DOMA by a margin of 52 to 34 percent.[83] The poll also asked about specific benefits currently off limits to same-sex couples because of DOMA. Of those polled, 60 percent believe same-sex couples should have access to Social Security survivor benefits,[84] while 64 percent support tax equity for same-sex couples.[85]

In July 2011, a bill to repeal DOMA, the appropriately named Respect for Marriage Act, was introduced in the US Senate. The first hearing held on the bill heard various witnesses testify about the discriminatory results of DOMA on same-sex, legally married couples. Their stories echo the problems faced by Edie Windsor and Thea Spyer.

Ron Wallen, a Californian who legally married his partner of fifty-five years in 2008, became unable to pay the mortgage on the house they shared after his husband died. He is unable to collect Social Security survivor benefits, unlike a member of a heterosexual couple, so he had to sell their home because he could no longer afford it.[86]

Susan and Karen Murray are a married couple in Vermont. Susan receives health insurance through her partner's employer-based insurance plan, but because they are not a heterosexual married couple, the value of the health insurance for Susan ($6,000) is considered taxable income for Karen, who has to pay income, FICA, and Medicare taxes on that amount.[87]

Andrew Sorbo from Connecticut lost his spouse to cancer in 2009. He was prohibited by DOMA from being covered by his partner's medical insurance plan through the federal government, so he had to purchase health insurance elsewhere at a much higher cost. He complained, "Last year, my insurance payments consumed almost a third of my $24,000 teacher pension."[88]

Such are the results of a statute that serves no real public policy or goal other than simply to punish people for who they are. As our population ages, and as same-sex marriage spreads to more states, cases like these will become commonplace. They offer real-life examples of the cruelty of this law and how it makes second-class citizens out of millions of Americans.

While the reaction from many Republicans to the Obama administration's announcement about its new policy on DOMA was strikingly muted, some social conservatives issued pro forma calls to stop the end of civilization as we know it.[89] Congressional Republicans like Representative Steve King from Iowa urged retaliation against the administration by chopping Justice Department budgets. Others urged Congress to step in with its own lawyers to defend DOMA, an unusual but legal option, and one Republican congressman, Lamar Smith of Texas, actually filed a suit to defend DOMA himself since the Department of Justice no longer wished to do so.[90]

Former Arkansas governor Mike Huckabee used the opportunity as a fund-raising ploy to "help defend marriage against the outrageous assault on our values,"[91] while former Speaker of the House Newt Gingrich, now on his third wife, issued a similar call to arms to protect traditional marriage. He even charged that President Obama's new stance on DOMA was an impeachable offense, although he later backed off that absurd claim.[92] Gingrich was proceeding with a then rocky campaign to win the 2012 Republican presidential nomination, so this issue offered another big club to him and like-minded presidential candidates to appeal to those Republican base voters adamantly opposed to changing the status quo when it comes to marriage or any kind of legal recognition for same-sex couples.

Other critics on the right also spoke out against the Obama administration's DOMA decision. Former governor of Alaska Sarah Palin wrote, "Like the majority of Americans, I support the Defense of Marriage Act and find it appalling that the Obama administration decided not to defend this federal law."[93] Apparently Palin was not at all aware that the majority of Americans do *not* support DOMA. Not to be outdone in his opposition to all things gay, Family Research Council president Tony Perkins attacked the Obama administration for shirking its legal duties, stating that "marriage as a male-female union has been . . . overwhelmingly supported by the American people."[94] He was ignorant as well (or at least pretending to be) of the polling that now shows a modest majority in favor of same-sex marriage rights.

Many Republicans, perhaps understandably, expressed great surprise and even outrage that the president would refuse to defend the constitutionality of a legally enacted statute, saying such a refusal conflicts with his oath of office. Even some who don't necessarily support DOMA have said the president has an official obligation to defend it in court. And yet a brief review of recent American presidents shows that such an action is not rare.

Presidents have taken such stands more than a dozen times since 2004, and many more times than that going back to the administrations of Harry S. Truman, Dwight D. Eisenhower, and John F. Kennedy. The Reagan administration, for example, refused to defend the independent counsel law, which the Supreme Court ruled was constitutional by a 7–1 majority.[95] He also chose not to defend a congressional resolution that vetoed a deportation order by the Immigration and Naturalization Service.[96]

The first Bush administration refused to defend the federal law mandating affirmative action in the assignment of broadcasting licenses, while the second Bush administration refused to defend a law that denied federal funds to local transit systems that allowed display ads urging drug legalization.[97] George W. Bush's administration also failed to defend a law prohibiting the display of ads from a marijuana-reform organization in public transportation systems.[98] His solicitor general, Paul Clement, said that the administration didn't have a viable argument for doing so. And the Clinton administration failed to defend a law that required dismissal of HIV-positive members of the armed forces.[99]

Clearly, not defending specific laws because they are considered unconstitutional is nothing new, despite the cries of feigned outrage from those who oppose the Obama administration's action. Even a hero of the conservative movement, former solicitor general Robert Bork, undertook a challenge to the 1971 Federal Election Campaign Act, which, as solicitor general, he was ostensibly required to defend. He instead filed a brief challenging a provision of that law, arguing that it would be "a betrayal of profound obligations to the Court and to Constitutional processes to take the simplistic position that whatever Congress enacts we will defend."[100]

Other conservative law professors have spoken out as well about the appropriateness of President Obama's decision. George Mason University professor Ilya Somin argued that "if a President genuinely believes that a federal statute is unconstitutional he has a duty *not* to defend it."[101] And John Yoo, the former Bush administration lawyer who justified many of the Bush administration's antiterrorist legal decisions, stated that Obama's decision was "justified under the Constitution's original allocation of authority to the President."[102] These are hardly knee-jerk leftists trying to usher in a sweeping new era of executive authority.

Surely, then, the charge by some conservatives that this action by the Obama administration was unprecedented is simply erroneous, not to mention hypocritical. It is also a bit self-defeating in the constraints such a stance puts on future Republican presidents. Imagine, for example, that a new Republican president takes office in 2013 and faces a court challenge on the constitutionality of Obamacare. Would conservatives who are now criticizing Obama for his position on DOMA take the same stance regarding a Republican president who refused to defend the health insurance law we all love to hate?

The answer to that question is self-evident. If Republicans are smart, they'll allow this issue to play out in the courts, where any issue regarding the constitutionality of a federal bill should play out. Republican candidates who can think beyond the short-term goal of winning over Republican base voters will not make it the centerpiece of their presidential campaigns because, as the polling data show, the American people are moving in a different direction.

The first legislative victory in the effort to repeal DOMA occurred in the Senate in late 2011 when the Respect for Marriage Act passed the Democrat-controlled Judiciary Committee in a 10–8 party-line vote. Unfortunately, even though DOMA directly attacks federalism by diminishing the right of the states to set their own marriage policies, not one Senate Republican opted to sponsor the bill. Little headway toward repealing this statute beyond this mostly symbolic committee vote is expected in 2012.

FEDERAL MARRIAGE AMENDMENT

Strongly related to DOMA is another federal attempt to overrule the traditional federalist position on marriage as a state issue, the Federal Marriage Amendment (FMA), first introduced in the House of Representative in 2003 by Representative Marilyn Musgrave from Colorado. It consisted of just two sentences: "Marriage in the United States shall consist only of the union of a man and a woman. Neither this Constitution or the constitution of any State, nor state or federal law, shall be construed to require that marital status of the legal incidents thereof be conferred upon unmarried couples or groups."[103] Written with the assistance of Judge Robert Bork and the Alliance for Marriage, this measure sought, in response to outrage about a recent Massachusetts Supreme Court decision legalizing same-sex marriage, to preempt the states' traditional control over this issue by amending the US Constitution to define marriage as strictly a union between a man and a woman.

Having gone nowhere in Congress in 2003, a revised version of the amendment was reintroduced in 2004 in both chambers.[104] Although it received a majority of House votes, it failed to reach the 290 votes required to pass a constitutional amendment. It also failed in the Senate, receiving only forty-eight votes out of the sixty required to invoke cloture, a motion to cut off debate and go to a vote. While it helped rally the Republican base during the presidential election, it also reinforced the growing perception of the Republican Party as obsessed with divisive social issues, despite Bush's narrow reelection victory.

Lost in the controversy surrounding the FMA and the anti-gay animus among many of the president's supporters was the fact that, for the first time ever, a Republican president had publicly stated he was not opposed to states enacting civil unions.[105] President Bush had in fact urged a version of the amendment that would have allowed states to pass such unions and even mentioned that position in a campaign speech just before Election Day in 2004.[106] It received little media coverage.

Having won the election, Republicans reintroduced the amendment in the new session of Congress, but it failed yet again by roughly the same margins as before, with twenty-seven Republicans voting against it in the House and eight Senate Republicans voting against the cloture motion to cut off debate.[107] Having now dutifully done the bidding of the Religious Right in making the issue a top legislative priority and campaigning on it in several elections, Republicans were soundly thumped in the 2006 election and lost both the House and the Senate.

A variety of polls about the FMA reveal substantial public opposition to it. A 2006 Quinnipiac University poll showed 53 percent of registered voters opposed, with 43 percent in favor.[108] Three major polls about the amendment were done in 2008. A May 2008 Gallup poll showed an even split, with 49 percent in favor and 48 percent opposed. An August poll by *Time* magazine showed 58 percent opposed, with just 35 percent in support.[109] Another Quinnipiac poll in July showed 56 percent opposed and 38 percent in favor.[110] Little polling has been done on the question since then, but given the major shift in public opinion about gay marriage, one can fairly surmise that opposition to the amendment is the same as or even greater than it was a few years ago.

Although few believe such an amendment has any serious chance of passing Congress, let alone being ratified by three-quarters of the states, some continue to use it as a tool to kowtow to the anti-gay Right, particularly Republican presidential candidates trying to appeal to the narrow base that is so influential in some of the state primaries and caucuses leading up to the nomination in 2012. Candidates Mitt Romney, Newt Gingrich, Tim Pawlenty, Michele Bachmann, Rick Perry, Herman Cain, and Rick Santorum all stated their support for a federal marriage amendment,[111] while Representative Ron Paul and former governors Jon Huntsman and Gary Johnson came out against it.[112]

IMMIGRATION RIGHTS FOR SAME-SEX COUPLES

One longtime benefit accorded to heterosexual couples in the United States is the right of a foreign national to gain legal residency in the United States by virtue of marrying an American citizen. Many thousands of foreign individuals have used this benefit to begin a new life in the United States. Unfortunately, even legally married same-sex couples are being denied this same right by means of the Defense of Marriage Act, which forces the federal government to ignore valid same-sex marriages when it comes to federal benefits and privileges. As a consequence, the number of cases in which a legally married spouse is awaiting deportation is growing.[113]

A married gay couple from San Francisco provides an example of how DOMA imposes a double standard on immigration cases. Bradford Wells and Anthony John Makk, a citizen of Australia, were married seven years ago in Massachusetts, where they enjoy the same legal rights and privileges as other married couples. But when Makk shut down his business to care for his partner, who is living with AIDS, he lost his visa. When he applied for permanent residency as the legal spouse of an American citizen, however, US Immigration and Customs Enforcement denied his claim, citing the requirements of DOMA. "The claimed relationship between the petitioner and the beneficiary is not a petitionable relationship," they were told. As a result, after a nineteen-year relationship and seven years of marriage, Makk could be deported at any time, leaving his sick husband to fend for himself.[114]

This is not an isolated case. Paul Wilson Dorman, a British citizen, has lived in the United States since 1996 in a fifteen-year committed relationship and entered into a civil union in 2009. Having never obtained a green card or citizenship, however, he was facing deportation until US Attorney General Eric Holder intervened by asking an immigration court to determine whether Dorman should be considered a spouse under the New Jersey law that granted the couple their civil union. His deportation is now temporarily on hold, but he faces an uncertain outcome.[115]

As does Henry Valandia, a Venezuelan citizen, who came to the United States in 2002 on a visitor's visa, which expired after six months. In an effort to prevent his mandated deportation, however, his legally married spouse, Josh Vandiver, a US citizen, applied for a green card. Since the US government does not recognize their Connecticut marriage, however, the application was denied. Fortunately for the couple, Valandia's deportation was halted based on the order by Attorney General Holder in the Dorman case.[116]

As with the other DOMA-related legal cases, the number of immigration-related cases will grow, potentially tearing apart other couples by denying them the same federal benefits that heterosexual couples routinely count on. Only the repeal of DOMA will prevent more examples of the effects of this apartheid-like law.

GAY ADOPTION

Parenting by gay singles or couples is a rapidly growing phenomenon in this country. In the United States, over a quarter of a million children are living with same-sex couples, and one-quarter of them are adopted.[117] In 2009, about nineteen thousand gay couples had adopted children.[118]

Laws governing adoption are primarily a state issue, but, surprisingly, there are almost no state prohibitions against gay adoption. Florida is the only state that until recently prohibited adoption by gay singles or couples. In 2008 a state judge struck that law down, saying it violated equal protection rights for both the children and the prospective parents. The state filed an appeal of that decision, but in a historic decision on September 22, 2010, a Florida appeals court ruled that the ban was unconstitutional. The court found "no rational basis" for the ban, and Florida's Department of Children and Families agreed as part of the ruling that "gay people and heterosexuals make equally good parents."[119] The state may still file an appeal to the state supreme court, but it appears likely that the country's most draconian anti-gay adoption law is now dead.[120]

In 2008, Arkansas voters passed Act 1, a measure that banned anyone "cohabitating outside of a valid marriage" from adopting a child or even becoming a foster parent, although the ban applied only to gay couples, not singles. Nevertheless, a state judge overturned the measure in 2010.[121]

Adoption law governing gay couples (rather than single parents) across the states is more problematic. Just eighteen states explicitly allow it, with most of the rest having either unclear policies or no explicit prohibition.[122] Only two states—Utah and Mississippi—explicitly prohibit it. Regulations in twenty-eight states allow same-sex partners to petition the courts to adopt their partner's child.[123]

Despite the active opposition to gay parenting by some conservatives, there is no evidence that gay parents are any less effective or loving than heterosexual ones, and numerous academic studies suggest that same-gender couples are still able to provide the proper role models that children need.[124]

The common argument made by social conservatives and others—that children are better off when raised in two-parent, male-and-female households—generally holds true in terms of children raised by single mothers. A whole host of economic and social measurements reveal the generally negative consequences of single motherhood, particularly among low-income women.

Unfortunately, some social conservatives extrapolate those negative consequences to make unwarranted conclusions about same-sex adoption, both by single gay parents and same-sex couples, but the comparison simply isn't germane. Many social conservatives deliberately confuse the two issues because they use the controversy about the negative consequences that can stem from single motherhood as another reason to oppose same-sex marriage and adoption by same-sex couples.

As anyone who has studied the issue knows, the breakdown of the modern American family and the large increase in the number of children born to single mothers began at least forty years ago, driven by the rise of the welfare state and policies that actually encouraged those on welfare to remain unmarried, even while bearing children. Virtually all of these children also became permanent wards of the state.

The African American community in particular was seduced by this process, and we are all now very familiar with the resulting social pathologies this welfare dependence has produced, from high rates of unemployment and violent crime to millions of fatherless children who get caught up in the criminal justice system and then begin the cycle all over again. Whites and other ethnic groups have also experienced a dramatic increase in the number of children born out of wedlock, with some of the same consequences, but the effects of those policies have been most devastating in the African American community.

Colbert King, a black columnist for the *Washington Post*, itemized some of the consequences of the welfare state in a March 6, 2011, column. In 1960, the black marriage rate was 61 percent.[125] By 2008, it had dropped to 32 percent.[126] In 2008, 72 percent of black women bearing children were unmarried.[127] Of black children, 52 percent are raised in single-parent households,[128] and only one-third are raised with two married parents.[129] None of this can even remotely be laid at the doorstep of gays and lesbians fighting for greater legal equality.

All conservatives and libertarians understand the pernicious effects that decades of government policies have had. Most of them also understand, however, that the way to curtail these negative consequences is to end the policies that produced them in the first place—for example, by reducing the financial incentives that welfare programs often provide to bear children out of wedlock.

Unfortunately, many social conservatives and organizations, such as the Family Research Council (FRC) and Focus on the Family, attempt to use these government-caused pathologies as a reason to oppose allowing gays and lesbians the same rights to a family structure as heterosexuals, including the right to adopt and to form civil unions or to marry. They argue that allowing gays and lesbians to adopt and raise families and giving them relationship rights will weaken the traditional two-parent family. They refuse to recognize, however, that the breakdown of the two-parent heterosexual family they lament was caused by heterosexuals shirking their responsibilities as parents and spouses, not by gay people asking for their rights.

Gay people did not cause the skyrocketing rate of divorce (and the ease of obtaining one). Gay people did not cause the sharp drop in marriage rates among heterosexuals. Gay people did not cause the rise of illegitimacy over the past forty years. And yet these social conservative organizations and some of their brethren on the right, including (ironically) many black ministers and their followers, argue that granting equal rights to gay couples and families will somehow have dire consequences for the already broken American family, particularly the black family. It's an intellectual bait-and-switch argument, but it's not fooling many people.

Writing in the February 7, 2011, edition of the *Los Angeles Times*, Cato Institute executive vice president David Boaz hit the nail on the head by pointing out that social conservatives are not offering solutions to real social ills like welfare dependency and the birth of millions of children out of wedlock by pushing an anti–gay rights agenda.[130] "Social conservatives say they're trying to address the problems of family breakdown, crime and welfare costs," according to Boaz, "but there's a huge disconnect between the problems they identify and the policy solutions they propose."[131] Crime, failing schools, high poverty rates, and drug and alcohol abuse are all serious social problems, he wrote, "but those problems have nothing to do with abortion or gay marriage, the issues that social conservatives talk most about. . . . And one thing gay couples are not doing is filling the world with fatherless children."[132]

Instead of focusing their efforts on fighting divorce and the low rate of marriage in minority communities by changing the policies responsible for these problems, social conservative organizations have instead become obsessed with homosexuality and turned their sites on it. Boaz laid the blame where it belongs:

> Take a look at the key issues on the website of the Family Research Council, the chief social conservative group. It recently listed eight

> papers on abortion and stem cells, seven on gays and gay marriage, and one on divorce. Nothing much has changed since 1994, when I reviewed the Council's publications index and found that the two categories with the most listings were "Homosexual" and "Homosexuality in the Military"—a total of 34 items (plus four on AIDS). The organization did show some interest in parenthood—nine items on family structure, 13 on parenthood, and six on pregnancy—but there were more items on homosexuality than on all of those issues combined. There was no listing for divorce. Since that time, the out-of-wedlock birthrate has risen from 32 percent to 40 percent.[133]

Talk about the FRC's misplaced priorities, unless of course the priority is simply promoting anti-gay animus!

The simple fact is this: Preventing gay couples from enjoying the same legal rights as heterosexual couples, including the freedom to raise families, will do nothing to reverse at least forty years of an epidemic of heterosexual divorce, illegitimacy, crime, and various other social ills we suffer from. Arguing that there is some connection between the two is intellectually dishonest and unconvincing.

There is clearly a double standard at work when it comes to the legal rights of single parents based on their sexual orientation. Although some argue, often with good reason, that single mothers or fathers can't do as good a job of raising kids as a couple might, no one has ever proposed prohibiting heterosexual single parenthood. Surely, gay singles and couples should have no fewer rights than single heterosexual parents.

Mainstream professional organizations representing social workers, psychologists, and doctors unanimously recognize both the ability and the right of gay parents to provide loving households. The American Academy of Pediatrics, the American Academy of Family Physicians, the National Association of Social Workers, the Child Welfare League, the American Psychological Association, and the American Medical Association all support same-sex adoption rights and oppose the suggestion by opponents that gay parents can't do as good a job,[134] especially in light of the great need for adoptive and foster parents in many states. And a large pool of peer-reviewed academic research about gay parents backs up their conclusions.[135] Unfortunately, some unsuspecting people are fooled by right-wing front groups like the American College of Pediatricians, an anti-gay fringe group set up to oppose same-sex adoption based on fake studies and doctored science.

Polls show that Americans generally favor the right of gay couples to adopt, a dramatic shift over the past thirty years. In 2007, both a CNN and a Gallup poll showed 57 percent supporting that right, with 40 percent opposed.[136] A 2009 Quinnipiac poll showed 53 percent in support.[137] While this support can vary widely state by state, the percentage of voters in favor of such rights continues to grow everywhere, especially in light of the fact that at least half a million children are looking for permanent homes every year.

For Republicans, the principles of equal protection and due process should clearly take precedence on this issue over any possible personal or religious discomfort with homosexuality. The right to set up family households, even if they differ from the norm, is a fundamental one that all Republicans should support. As with other gay issues, instilling the party with a new sense of social tolerance can only help the party win the support it needs from independent and younger voters.

CONCLUSION

The nine issues just discussed—ENDA; public-sector employment protections; hate crime legislation; Don't Ask, Don't Tell; state sodomy laws; the Defense of Marriage Act; the Federal Marriage Amendment; immigration; and gay adoption—can and should be resolved based on traditional Republican principles of equal protection under the law and individual rights. Every one of these issues has substantial majority support (including, in most cases, majority Republican support), sometimes by very large margins. Given the generational divide on these issues, public support for gay rights will continue to grow. Unless they wish to be left behind, it's time for Republican leaders and candidates to begin to reflect the more socially tolerant views of not just the American people but also most Republican voters.

4

THE THORNY ISSUE OF GAY MARRIAGE

Same-sex marriage has frightened and enraged opponents of gay rights more than any other issue. It's so charged with emotion and symbolism on both sides that we all need to pause, take a deep breath, and analyze the issues involved in a calm and rational manner. Here is a brief review of the events that brought us to where we are today in this debate.

Few people either inside or outside the gay community had ever seriously discussed marriage rights until the 2003 *Goodridge v. Department of Public Health* decision that legalized same-sex marriage in Massachusetts. One of the first, and perhaps the most prominent, exceptions was Andrew Sullivan, a gay conservative who was then editor at the *New Republic*, a liberal opinion magazine based in Washington, DC. In 1989, Sullivan penned a piece titled "Here Comes the Groom: A Conservative Case for Gay Marriage,"[1] in which he argued that grafting a conservative social institution such as marriage onto the gay and lesbian communities would help provide the same stability and security it does to heterosexual families. Some in the gay community have vilified Sullivan and other gay advocates of same-sex marriage for selling out the gay community by supporting marriage and thereby reinforcing patriarchy and other alleged evils of capitalist society. Ironically, this issue has created an odd alliance of Far Left and Far Right in their joint opposition to marriage equality.

The first high-profile legal case involving same-sex marriage took place in Hawaii in 1993,[2] when the state's supreme court ruled that Hawaii's law against same-sex marriage was unconstitutional unless there was a compelling state interest in banning it. Before the ruling could take effect, in 1998, Hawaiians voted overwhelmingly to amend the state constitution to give the legislature the power to restrict marriage to opposite-sex couples only. That remains the law today.

The Hawaii case prompted a swift reaction from the federal government. In 1996, Congress overwhelmingly passed the Defense of Marriage Act (DOMA), which formally defined marriage for federal government purposes as a union between one man and one woman.[3] DOMA also denied federal benefits for same-sex couples and relieved states of any legal obligation to recognize same-sex marriages performed in other states. Most Democrats and virtually all Republicans voted for DOMA as it passed the Senate by an 85–14 vote and the House by a 342–67 margin.[4] President Bill Clinton signed the measure into law. The law did not change or affect state laws regarding marriage, and some may have thought (or hoped) that it would end the increasingly contentious issue.

Things remained quiet on the marriage equality front until 2003, when the national debate on this issue reignited. The spark was a lawsuit in Massachusetts. In the *Goodridge* case, the Massachusetts Supreme Judicial Court declared that state's law against same-sex marriage violated the state constitution.[5] The ruling made Massachusetts only the sixth jurisdiction in the world at the time to permit same-sex marriage, along with the Netherlands, Belgium, Ontario, British Columbia, and Quebec (since then, Argentina, Canada, Iceland, Norway, South Africa, Spain, Sweden, and Portugal have legalized same-sex marriage). In the United States, the District of Columbia and six other states have also instituted same-sex marriage: Connecticut, Iowa, New Hampshire, Vermont, Washington, and New York (the largest state so far). In 2009, Maine's legislature adopted gay marriage, but the state's voters overturned that law within months.

Subsequent attempts in Massachusetts to overturn the court's decision failed when the state legislature voted in 2007 against putting a repeal measure on the ballot, effectively giving gay marriage in that state the legislature's seal of approval. Even many original opponents of gay marriage in Massachusetts have changed their minds. Massachusetts now has sixteen thousand gay married couples,[6] and yet, contrary to predictions by opponents of gay marriage, divorce rates in Massachusetts have dropped and are now the lowest in the country.[7]

In March 2004, San Francisco city officials began issuing marriage licenses to same-sex couples in violation of California state law. Over three thousand couples married before the California Supreme Court declared the marriages null and void.[8] Media coverage of these San Francisco marriages was intense, and the national reaction to both them and the Massachusetts court decision was swift and furious. In 2004, thirteen states voted to ban gay marriage at the ballot box.[9] The narrowest margin of victory was in Oregon, with 57 percent in favor; in states like Kentucky, Georgia, and Arkansas, the ban passed by more than three to one, and in Mississippi, it passed by six to one. It was not surprising that something as shocking and new to the average American provoked such a strong response. Anti–gay rights organizations such as the Family Research Council, Focus on the Family, and the American Family Association crowed about the wins. And it wasn't just marriage that was banned; some states also banned civil unions and domestic partnerships.

Coming on the heels of the Massachusetts court decision, the San Francisco marriages fueled the calls for the Federal Marriage Amendment, which would have written the definition of "traditional" marriage into the US Constitution and barred states from adopting marriage equality, even if done democratically at the ballot box or legislatively by state lawmakers. Although this proposal became the top national priority of anti–gay rights groups, it failed in two attempts to gain enough Republican votes in the US Senate and effectively died in 2006,[10] even before Democrats took control of the Senate in November of that year, killing any chance that the amendment would be reconsidered. Few Senate Republicans have any interest in refighting a lost battle heading into the 2012 election, although most of the Republican presidential field still supported such a measure, including Mitt Romney, Rick Santorum, Michele Bachmann, Tim Pawlenty, Herman Cain, Newt Gingrich, and Rick Perry.[11]

More gay marriage bans followed the first round in 2004, although with smaller margins of victory. Twenty-nine states now have constitutional bans on gay marriage, while nine others have statutes that outlaw it.[12] Although some of these states, such as California, have strong (almost marriage-like) protections for same-sex couples, most do not, and at least nineteen of the states that prohibit gay marriage also prohibit any legal recognition of gay couples.[13] Three states—New York, Maryland, and Rhode Island—recognize out-of-state gay marriages, but same-sex unions cannot be performed in Maryland or Rhode Island.

The architects of state marriage bans have, for the most part, been socially conservative and Religious Right voters and leaders associated with the Republican Party, although black pastors have helped lead the fight in some states and the District of Columbia. The Massachusetts court decision has proved a financial boon to their organizations, and although opposition to gay marriage has waned considerably over the past few years,[14] Religious Right leaders have been effective at exploiting voters' confusion and anger about same-sex marriage.

There are three important issues to consider in this debate:

1. the merits and justice of same-sex marriage or other forms of relationship recognition;
2. the position of the American people in general and Republicans in particular regarding legal recognition of same-sex couples; and
3. the best process for obtaining same-sex marriage: through the courts, the state legislature, the ballot box, or all three.

WHAT'S WRONG WITH SAME-SEX MARRIAGE?

Some opponents of same-sex marriage are so emotionally and unalterably opposed to homosexuality and gay unions that it's not really possible to have a rational discussion about the issue. But for everyone else, any discussion must begin with the recognition that there is both a civil and a religious component to marriage, and each is very different.

The marriage license is the civil part of marriage and has nothing to do with religion or church in any legal sense. It is a government license allowing two people to join in the marriage contract. Obtaining the license requires no religious belief, of course, and no intent to produce offspring: it makes no mention of either. To complete the marriage process, two people need only find a justice of the peace or some other legally sanctioned person to conduct the ceremony. The marriage license doesn't even require that both parties love one another. It is, totally and completely, a document that simply binds two people together from a legal perspective, be they Christian, atheist, or anything else. Proponents of marriage equality focus on this aspect of marriage: equal access for same-sex couples to the license and the many benefits that come with it. This includes not just the stability and security of a stable, legally protected relationship but also the monetary benefits and numerous legal protections as well. The US Government Accounting Office lists 1,138 legal rights, monetary benefits, and responsibilities that come with marriage,[15] all now denied to both unmarried straight and same-sex couples, from tax equity (excluding health insurance benefits from taxable income) to spousal Social Security benefits.

The other major aspect of marriage is religious in nature. This is the ceremonial part of marriage that usually takes place in a church or temple, although millions do not participate in this aspect of marriage when they tie the proverbial knot. Marriage, of course, has immense religious significance to people of faith, although its meaning and significance varies greatly from religion to religion and especially from culture to culture. The religious aspect of marriage is clearly secondary from a legal perspective, however, because it is not required in order to execute a marriage; only a marriage license and a justice of the peace are required to do that. A couple can have the most elaborate and meaningful religious ceremony possible, and many do, but that ceremony and the church's blessing are neither necessary nor sufficient to execute a legally recognized marriage. Many religious people have labeled marriage a "holy union" before God, but such a belief or description has no legal standing whatsoever—nor should it.

The first reaction of most opponents of gay marriage is to raise various religious objections to both homosexuality and same-sex unions. Apart from the important fact that some Christian denominations (such as Episcopalians, the United Church of Christ, Quakers, some Methodists, Unitarians, and others) sanction same-sex unions, these opponents are forgetting that the marriage license is a civil, not a religious, document. It favors no particular religious group or its views on homosexuality. It is not a stamp of approval—only a permission slip, if you will, to get married. Religious arguments against extending it to same-sex couples should be irrelevant in a country that boasts freedom of religion.

Other opponents of same-sex marriage say the primary purpose of marriage is procreation, but that is clearly false for millions of married people. The marriage license contains no requirement whatsoever to produce children, and in fact, no religion makes procreation a requirement for receiving its blessing or participating in its sacraments. Millions of heterosexuals in this country who have no intention of procreating, or who are too old or unable to do so, obtain their marriage licenses, get married, and receive the blessing of their respective churches.

The marriage license also mandates no belief in God, and, certainly, thousands of nonbelievers get married every year, illustrating yet again the nonreligious nature of civil marriage. Perhaps that is why the activists in the ranks of the Religious Right want a theocracy. They realize America is a secular state under which we have no religious requirements to hold office: we have mostly secular citizens as elected leaders—not ministers, priests, rabbis, or mullahs.

Opponents of marriage equality sometimes fall back on the "tradition" argument: marriage, they say, has always been between one man and one woman, and we should therefore not redefine it. But again, that is historically inaccurate. Polygamy was referred to, but not condemned, throughout the Old Testament, and as conservative *New York Times* columnist Ross Douthat has pointed out, "The default family arrangement in many cultures, modern as well as ancient, has been polygamy, not monogamy." Nor is "lifelong heterosexual monogamy obviously natural in the way that most Americans understand the term," he writes. "If 'natural' is defined to mean 'congruent with our biological instincts,' it's arguably one of the more unnatural arrangements imaginable."[16] Perhaps this fact explains the widespread polygamy, adultery, and even harems common in cultures around the world throughout human history, as well as today.

Marriage has, in fact, been a continuously evolving institution. Only in the sixteenth century, for example, did marriage begin to resemble what we have today—that is, one man united to one woman. Even then, marriages were often arranged by the families of the bride and groom, and women traditionally had few, if any, legal rights in the relationship. They were essentially property, first of their fathers and then of their husbands, and they were expected to do what they were told. And they did. Child brides were common, and marriages were more often about social status and political power than the idealized holy matrimony that today's "defenders" of marriage romanticize about.

By the time of the Reformation in the sixteenth century, most Protestants saw little reason for church involvement with marriage, which was considered more the purview of the state than the church. Martin Luther himself wrote, "Since marriage has existed from the beginning of the world and is still found among unbelievers, there is no reason why it should be called a sacrament of the New Law and of the church alone."[17] Marriage was becoming primarily an institution of government regarding its legal basis and whatever contractual rights it included.

The rise of classical liberalism, the philosophical ancestor of modern libertarianism, cemented this quite radical change, which, according to evangelical author John Witte, emphasized the contractual and consensual nature of marriage. Exponents of this view, he writes, "advocated the abolition of much that was considered . . . sacred in the Western legal tradition of marriage. They urged the abolition of the requirements of parental consent, church consecration, and formal witnesses for marriage. They questioned the exalted status of heterosexual monogamy, suggesting that such matters be left to private negotiation. They called for the absolute equality of husband and wife to receive, hold, and alienate property, to enter into contracts and commerce, to participate on equal terms in the workplace and in the public square. They castigated the state for leaving annulment practice to the church, and urged that the laws of annulment and divorce be both merged and expanded under exclusive state jurisdiction."[18]

The argument, then, that modern marriage is primarily a religious sacrament is false: a religious sacrament has no legal basis. Only the civil aspect of marriage has a legal foundation, which is the marriage license and the legal rights inherent in it.

That legal foundation continues to change. As recently as 1967, for example, interracial marriages in the United States were illegal, often based on the rationale that the scriptures forbade such unions, the same argument we hear today about same-sex unions. Only when the Supreme Court intervened in the case of *Loving v. Virginia* were state laws banning such marriages overturned. Would the current opponents of same-sex marriage who rail about judges getting involved in the same-sex marriage debate have damned the Supreme Court's 9–0 decision in this case as "judicial activism"? It's doubtful. In fact, that brilliantly argued decision states that marriage is a "basic civil right. . . . The freedom to marry, or not marry, a person of another race resides with the individual and cannot be infringed by the State."[19] The fundamental justice behind that decision is universal and provides the basis and rationale for legalizing same-sex marriage.

The often-heard argument that marriage as we know it is "under attack" because of the effort to legalize same-sex marriage is really inexplicable. It is bizarre to believe that allowing the small fraction of the population that would participate in same-sex marriage to do so would somehow pose a danger to the overwhelmingly heterosexual nature of the institution. How is granting to same-sex couples the same legal rights that come with the marriage license any threat at all to heterosexual marriage? In fact, many argue that spreading the institution of marriage to previously excluded gay couples would only strengthen it and widen its appeal.

Surely, with the high rate of divorce and declining rate of heterosexual marriage in the United States, the institution of marriage could use some help. Clearly, its decline, which has been going on for at least forty years, has had nothing to do with the recent emergence of same-sex marriage.

Addressing the real causes of the breakdown of the heterosexual family would seem a much better target for those who spend their time and money opposing same-sex marriage. Government statistics show that 40 percent of children today are born out of wedlock to heterosexual parents[20] (70 percent among blacks).[21] Yet much of the Religious Right is obsessed with homosexuality and the prospect of same-sex marriage. Wouldn't these opponents be wiser to tend to the systematic breakdown of heterosexual marriage caused by . . . heterosexuals?

The fact is that the popularity of marriage as an institution has dropped drastically over the past sixty years. According to the US Census Bureau, married-couple households now constitute less than half of the households in the United States.[22] In 1950, married couples made up over 78 percent of American households; today, that number has dropped to 49.7 percent. There are various reasons for this dramatic change, but the fact is that social mores and values are very different than they were sixty years ago. As much as religious fundamentalists might like to, America is not going back to what some might consider "the good old days." Trying to force-feed certain cultural and religious values to the American public, through legal sanctions and preferences, is both destined to fail and distinctly un-American. As social values continue to evolve, traditional Christians really have no choice but to evolve with them. They might not like the inevitable social change that is taking place, but in a free society, their only legitimate response can be to proselytize, not persecute.

Out of desperation, some opponents of marriage equality raise the specter of their churches and ministers being forced to sanction same-sex couples if we legalize same-sex marriage. The prospect of a fundamentalist denomination or the Catholic Church being forced to recognize or perform such marriages must be truly frightening to many people. But the spokesmen who use such imaginary threats to raise money and frighten their parishioners must realize these scary scenarios are completely fictional.

No credible proponent of marriage equality has ever proposed empowering the government to force any religious institution to sanction, recognize, or perform gay marriages (or even to admit gay members). In fact, those states that permit such marriages have specific legal guarantees against such imaginary threats. No church or minister in any state that now has gay marriage can honestly claim otherwise, and it's time opponents of same-sex marriage stop lying about this nonexistent threat.

Marriage equality threatens no one's freedom of religion; in fact, it's the churches that support marriage equality that have had their freedom of religion stripped away by the existing gay marriage bans. As stated earlier, many churches and denominations, after all, support same-sex marriage, and yet they are forbidden from performing or recognizing such unions by the constitutional and statutory bans that exist in most states. Some states, such as Texas and Virginia, even forbid such churches from performing same-sex "marriage" commitment ceremonies, even though the union has no legal basis because the couple lacks a marriage license. A clearer violation of religious liberty cannot be imagined.

WHERE DO THE AMERICAN PEOPLE AND REPUBLICANS STAND ON MARRIAGE?

Until recently, the Religious Right was mostly correct when it claimed that most Americans oppose same-sex marriage, although support and opposition varied widely by state as well as by demographic group. The Gallup poll from May 2010, for example, showed that 53 percent of Americans opposed gay marriage, while 44 percent supported it.[23] That was a significant change from just five years earlier, when those numbers were 62 and 32 percent, respectively.[24] And just sixteen years ago, in 1996,

68 percent opposed gay marriage while just 27 percent supported it.[25] The trend line of growing support for same-sex marriage has been clear for some time, and no one seriously expects that trend to change.

Polls from 2009 alone demonstrate the evolution in public opinion. An NBC/*Wall Street Journal* poll from October showed 41 percent in favor of same-sex marriage and 49 percent opposed,[26] which was then the lowest level of opposition in fourteen years. While a Quinnipiac poll from that same year showed just 38 percent in support with 55 percent opposed,[27] an April 30, 2009, ABC News/*Washington Post* poll showed 49 percent in support with 46 percent opposed.[28] Public opinion was clearly beginning to change, perhaps due in part to all the publicity garnered by the 2008 Proposition 8 vote in California and subsequent court battle.

That shift began to accelerate in 2010, with a small but consistent majority developing in favor of same-sex marriage according to most major pollsters. An August 2010 Associated Press poll, for example, revealed a 52 percent majority in favor of the government giving legal recognition to marriage between same-sex couples, with 46 percent opposed.[29] This included 25 percent of Republicans.[30]

A March 2011 ABC News/*Washington Post* poll showed a slim majority, 53 percent, in favor of same-sex marriage, with 47 percent opposed,[31] a complete reversal in just two years. While a March 2011 poll from Pew Research Center showed the nation evenly split, 45 percent in favor of same-sex marriage with 46 percent opposed,[32] an April CNN poll showed a 51 to 47 percent majority in favor.[33] And a Gallup poll in May 2011 showed a 53 to 45 percent majority.[34] A consistent pattern of support had clearly emerged, surprising even advocates.

Several polls later in the year demonstrated continuing growth in support for same-sex marriage. An August poll by the Associated Press and the National Constitution Center found that 53 percent of Americans supported marriage equality, a slight increase from the previous year.[35] Another poll by the Public Religion Research Institute (PRRI) showed the country evenly divided at 47 percent each, the first time in the PRRI poll that support for same-sex marriage was not a minority position. It also showed nearly a third (31 percent) of Republicans in support, 49 percent of Republican Millennials (ages eighteen to twenty-nine) in support, and even 44 percent of evangelical Millennials.[36] Finally, a Pew Research Center poll in November revealed a plurality of 46 percent supporting gay marriage, with 44 percent opposed.[37] This was a switch from just ten months earlier, when a plurality of respondents opposed same-sex marriage. Polling in 2012 will no doubt show that support for same-sex marriage continues to grow.

Not only is support for gay marriage growing across the board, but the intensity of support is also increasing; at the same time, the intensity of opposition is decreasing. An analysis of marriage polling numbers released on July 27, 2011, by pollsters Joel Benenson from the Benenson Strategy Group and Jan van Lohuizen from Voter Consumer Research revealed that their "survey of historical data shows that intensity of opinion is shifting as well. Where previously opponents of marriage for same-sex couples held their views more strongly than marriage supporters, this is no longer the case. Support has not just grown, it has intensified as well."[38] For example, the ABC News/*Washington Post* poll showed that "strong" support for gay marriage had increased by twelve points since 2004, while "strong" opposition had dropped by thirteen points.[39] Since 2004, Pew's "strongly favor" numbers were up by twelve points;[40] the "strongly oppose" side was down ten points.[41] The authors say that supporters now equal marriage opponents in their intensity of support. They also conclude that Americans are in the process of rethinking their views on the issue and that this support for same-sex marriage will sharply increase in the coming years, particularly because of the overwhelming support for it among younger Americans.

If the current rate of change in public opinion continues, by the 2012 national election, voters will favor gay marriage by a margin of 56 to 40 percent,[42] a very substantial majority in favor of marriage equality. It should be clear to even die-hard opponents that public opinion on this issue has changed quicker than anyone imagined and that support will only grow, given the differences in opinion between young and old. No one can now credibly argue that the courts or state legislatures are "imposing" same-sex marriage on an unwilling majority.

Some Far Right groups, however, simply will not accept reality. The Alliance Defense Fund (ADF), for example, conducted its own "poll" on the issue using a rent-a-poll firm called Public Opinion Strategies. This May 2011 poll asked fifteen hundred adults nationwide if they agreed with the following statement: "I believe marriage should be defined ONLY as a union between one man and one woman." According to the ADF, 62 percent of the respondents agreed with this statement,[43] and so it concluded they opposed same-sex marriage. The fact that this "poll" diverges so significantly from every recent reputable poll should raise red flags about its accuracy—and for good reason.

As critics of the poll have pointed out, it asked for the personal beliefs of the respondents, unlike other polls that ask about what public policy or the law should be. For example, the ABC News/*Washington Post* poll referred to earlier asked respondents, "Do you think it should be legal or illegal for gay and lesbian couples to get married?"[44] A majority said it should be legal. Likewise, the Pew Research Center poll asked, "Do you favor or oppose allowing gays and lesbians to marry legally?"[45] Respondents were evenly split, at 45 and 46 percent, respectively.[46] Real pollsters know that respondents may have a personal view of what constitutes marriage, but it may be very different from what they believe the law should be.

In fact, we've seen this kind of split opinion between personal beliefs as opposed to what should be legal on other controversial issues. According to a 2011 poll by the Public Religion Research Institute, 52 percent of Americans said abortion is morally wrong, yet 56 percent in the same poll said it should be legal in all or most cases.[47] As all pollsters know, including the one used by the Alliance Defense Fund, the wording they use is critical to the results they get. Clearly, the ADF purchased its poll and got the results it paid for and expected. They certainly are not representative of where Americans are now on this issue, or will be, but you can be sure the opponents will milk this "poll" for all its worth, the truth be damned. Other anti–gay rights groups, like the Family Research Council, quickly picked up and disseminated these "poll" results, which will no doubt be used to rally the troops and raise money for some time as "proof" that "radical homosexual activists" are forcing their agenda upon an unwilling nation.

Despite the growing support for marriage equality among the general population, support among Republicans and conservatives is, not surprisingly, considerably lower, even though it is also growing rapidly. A Pew Research poll from October 2010 showed support for marriage at 24 percent among Republicans,[48] while the more recent one in 2011 showed virtually the same result, a quarter of Republicans in favor.[49] The March 2011 ABC/*Washington Post* poll showed 31 percent of Republicans in support,[50] while a Public Religion Research Institute poll from May 2011 showed an astounding 37 percent of GOP voters in favor of marriage equality.[51]

As the polling clearly indicates, a growing number of Republicans and conservatives support gay marriage, from Laura Bush to Glenn Beck to Dennis Miller to Dick Cheney, and many more.[52] Even with this growing Republican support for marriage equality, however, civil unions and domestic partnerships draw much wider GOP support. Although they don't afford the same legal protections and privileges as marriage, civil unions and domestic partnerships offer at least some (and, in some cases, most) of the relationship rights offered by marriage. According to a 2009 Pew Research poll, almost half of Republicans, 48 percent, supported civil unions, including a third of the Republicans who opposed gay marriage.[53] A CBS News poll in August 2010 showed 59 percent of Republicans supporting either same-sex marriage or civil unions (25 percent for marriage, 34 percent for civil unions),[54] while a May 2011 poll from Public Policy Polling showed 51 percent in support of civil unions or marriage equality.[55] The common perception, then, that there is little or no support for relationship recognition among Republicans is flatly wrong, despite their general reticence about same-sex marriage.

Thirteen states that currently prohibit gay marriage recognize instead civil unions or domestic partnerships, including California, Nevada, Colorado, Hawaii, Maine, New Jersey, Oregon, Washington, Delaware, Wisconsin, Rhode Island, Maryland, and (most recently) Illinois.[56] Fully 57 percent of all Americans now support civil unions, according to both a 2009 Quinnipiac poll and a 2009 Pew Research poll.[57] A CBS/*New York Times* poll from April 2010 showed an overwhelming 63 percent in favor of either same-sex marriage or civil unions, with just 30 percent opposed to any legal recognition for gay couples.[58] And a Zogby poll from July 2011 showed an astonishing 70 percent of Americans favoring civil unions.[59]

Clearly, the broader appeal of civil unions and domestic partnerships offers a viable alternative to same-sex marriage in those states where marriage equality simply does not have sufficient public support to be a realistic option for state legislators, which is certainly a majority of the states. That is especially true for Republicans who support some form of relationship recognition but cannot or do not support full marriage equality. Republicans who at the very least support civil unions or domestic partnerships are clearly not voices in the wilderness anymore: they are a majority of rank-and-file Republicans, and they represent the future of the Republican Party.

Virtually every political analyst agrees that if the Republican Party is to maintain long-term political power at the national level, certainly in our most populous states, it will need to appeal to the moderates, independents, and younger voters who came back to the Republican Party in a big way in the 2010 midterm elections.[60] These groups support civil unions or marriage for gay couples at significantly higher rates than Republicans. Independents, for example, supported a constitutional right to marry for same-sex couples by a 57 percent majority in the August 2010 CNN poll,[61] while the March 2011 ABC/*Washington Post* poll showed 58 percent of independents in support.[62] These are the voters who are essential to continued Republican electoral success.

Columbia University political scientists Jeffrey Lax and Justin Phillips argue that there is a thirty-five point gap on the issue between those under thirty and those over sixty-five.[63] The implications of those numbers for Republicans are enormous. "If policy were set by state-by-state majorities of those 65 or older, none would allow same-sex marriage," Lax reported in 2009.[64] However, "if policy were set by those under 30, only 12 states would *not* allow same-sex marriage."[65] This is a striking generational difference. As strongly as they may feel about the issue, the opponents of same-sex marriage are spitting into the wind when it comes to the future of gay marriage in America, especially since support for it will only grow among younger voters.

Even some on the right who oppose marriage equality are beginning to realize their opposition may ultimately be a lost cause. Jim Daly, CEO of the anti–gay rights group Focus on the Family, recently lamented the growing support for marriage equality: "We're losing on that one, especially among the 20- and 30-somethings: 65 to 70 percent of them favor same-sex marriage. I don't know if that's going to change with a little more age—demographers would say probably not. We've probably lost that. I don't want to be extremist here, but I think we need to start calculating where we are in the culture."[66] Amen to that.

This is why Republicans would be wise to look to the future rather than the past. As Steve Schmidt, Senator John McCain's senior strategist during his 2008 presidential campaign, said after their losing race, "The Republican Party is shrinking. One of the reasons it is shrinking is because there are large demographics in the country that view the [Republican] party as intolerant and not relevant to them. Politics is about addition."[67] Since Barack Obama came to office, of course, support for Republicans has surged, primarily because moderates and independents have deserted the Democrats and their policies of government-directed health care, high debt, and continuous bailouts and subsidies for big business and special interests. The 2010 election results merely confirmed what most political analysts knew: most of the swing voters who gave the Democrats their victories in 2006 and 2008 have swung back to Republicans.[68]

This increasing support for the GOP will not last, however, if Republicans continue to allow the Religious Right to impose an anti–gay rights agenda on the party. The independents and moderates who are returning to the Republican Party are doing so because of economic issues and the Republican Party's perceived superiority in that area. Polls consistently show that these same voters are generally pro–gay rights and completely opposed to the extreme anti–gay rights agenda of the Religious Right.

In fact, in the three most notable Republican electoral comebacks between the 2008 presidential election and the 2010 midterm election, there was notable support for expanding gay rights, helping bring back the moderates and independents who had been deserting the party in droves.

In New Jersey in 2009, Governor Chris Christie supported civil unions, as did Senator Scott Brown from Massachusetts in his historic special-election win in early 2010. Both men have gone on to publicly express support for expanding gay and lesbian rights since their respective elections, with Senator Brown being one of just eight Republican senators voting to repeal the Pentagon's discriminatory Don't Ask, Don't Tell policy.

In Virginia in 2009, Republican governor Bob McDonnell repeatedly expressed support during his campaign for employment nondiscrimination on the basis of sexual orientation, even stating that gays have a constitutional right to equality, positions unheard of from previous

Republican candidates for any statewide office in Virginia. He won with 57 percent of the vote, and since taking office, Governor McDonnell has issued an executive directive mandating a policy of employment nondiscrimination on the basis of sexual orientation for state employees. While that directive doesn't go far enough, it represents a distinct change from the governor's previous public stands on gay rights.

Governor McDonnell and all Virginia Republicans, in fact, would be wise to remember that the independents who put them back in office in 2009 opposed Virginia's 2006 marriage amendment by a 53 to 47 percent majority.[69] In fact, a May 2011 *Washington Post*/ABC News poll showed that a substantial plurality of Virginians, 47 percent, now support same-sex marriage, with 43 percent opposed.[70] Support for same-sex marriage included 53 percent of independents and even 40 percent of Republicans in that same poll.[71] Statewide polls conducted the same year as Virginia's marriage amendment showed even then a majority of voters in favor of civil unions. Social mores are rapidly changing, even in Virginia.

Libertarian Republicans should be especially outspoken in their support for either marriage equality or civil unions, because they can be very effective in explaining to their fellow Republicans not only the political advantages of social tolerance but also why it is consistent with core conservative and libertarian political values.

Admittedly, promoting or defending marriage equality is often difficult for Republican candidates, even if they believe it is ultimately the right position to take. Supporting civil unions, however, at least allows them to position themselves as more socially tolerant while still giving heterosexual-only marriage a special status, thus putting them in a stronger electoral position vis-à-vis Democrat opponents who more broadly favor gay rights.

Morally, it can be troubling to support a form of second-class citizenship that some say characterizes civil unions, but no one can deny that they would nonetheless be a big improvement compared to no relationship recognition at all. Unfortunately, social progress sometimes comes in giant leaps and sometimes just in small steps. Given the lack of any relationship recognition for gay couples in most states, civil unions would be a big step forward. Therefore, they are worth supporting and fighting for if same-sex marriage is simply unattainable.

HOW DO WE GET THERE?

Given the modest majority support for same-sex marriage and the overwhelming public support for civil unions, what's the best way to get to legal equality? Ideally, of course, voters would approve measures repealing the constitutional and statutory bans on gay marriage, or at least amend them to permit civil unions or similar legal arrangements, and we may soon see the beginning of that process in some states. Several proposed state constitutional amendments banning gay marriage will be on the ballot in 2012, including in Minnesota and North Carolina, and they will test whether this modest majority support for marriage equality can be translated into electoral defeats for these amendments. Only once, in Arizona, has such an amendment been defeated, and it later passed after its scope was narrowed.

The question of whether fundamental rights should even be subject to majority rule, however, is a very important one, just as is the role of the courts in protecting liberty.

Many conservatives adhere to a theory of constitutional jurisprudence often called "original intent," which refers to the intent of the original Founding Fathers (or what some think they intended) as expressed by the specific wording they used in composing the text of the Constitution. Former attorney general Edwin Meese explained in 1985 that the theory means judges should exhibit "a deeply rooted commitment to the idea of democracy,"[72] and his perspective was a response to several decades of what had been called "judicial activism" on the Supreme Court under Chief Justice Earl Warren and other modern liberals. Meese and other conservatives correctly saw these justices as imposing their personal political beliefs rather than applying the law or following the original intentions of the Founding Fathers, the result often being a larger and more intrusive federal government.

A related conservative legal philosophy is "strict constructionism," which has generally referred to a narrow judicial interpretation of what the Founding Fathers meant when using a particular phrase or word. Yet Supreme Court Justice Antonin Scalia has argued that constitutional text should not be construed either strictly or leniently, but "reasonably, to contain all that it fairly means."[73] In other words, conservatives object when Court decisions are used to subjectively legislate, yet they promote a process that entails subjective determinations by the Court of what is "reasonable," contrary to their own conservative mantras against judicial activism.

Unfortunately, the Founders' intent is not always as clear as many conservatives would have you believe. Moreover, many modern conservative defenders of the Constitution seem to have missed the parts about liberty and the separation of powers, which are so integral to the Constitution. Too often, they fail to see the wisdom of the courts as a sorely needed check on legislative and executive power rather than as a rubber stamp for it. The Constitution is not just a framework for governance; it is also a framework for preserving liberty.

As Damon Root incisively wrote in the July 2010 issue of *Reason* magazine, "Most supporters of ratification understood the judicial power as including the authority to decide whether acts of Congress were consistent with the Constitution,"[74] and to declare them null and void if they were not. That may be "judicial activism," but it is the right kind of activism, which strikes down unjust laws to preserve freedom.

Regrettably, modern conservatives have often strayed from the Constitution. Consider, for example, former federal appeals court judge (and Ronald Reagan nominee for the Supreme Court) Robert Bork, who is perhaps the most notable spokesman for the conservative point of view. Bork's belief in almost untrammeled majority rule is legendary. In many ways, he has repudiated the constitutional views that most conservatives (and certainly all libertarians) held for many years about the nature of rights and the Constitution's role in protecting them. For example, both Bork and his intellectual soulmate, Supreme Court Justice Antonin Scalia, have explicitly repudiated the basis for economic freedom outlined in the famous 1905 Supreme Court decision in *Lochner v. New York*, which overturned a state law regulating the hours of workers in a New York bakery. That decision, among others, was a bulwark against the growth of government and its control over economic freedom under Progressivism and the New Deal until it was eventually overridden by other Supreme Court decisions.

Bork and Scalia have attacked that decision and repudiated the fundamental protections afforded to both economic freedom and personal liberty by the Fourteenth Amendment. In Bork's view, the *Loch-*

ner decision is "the symbol, indeed the quintessence, of judicial usurpation of power."[75] Damon Root explained, "As Bork sees it, the 'first principle' of the American system isn't the protection of individual rights. 'In wide areas of life,' he writes in *The Tempting of America*, 'majorities are entitled to rule, if they wish, simply because they are majorities.' That means that in the vast majority of cases, the courts should give lawmakers the benefit of the doubt and presume the constitutionality of the disputed law, including economic regulations."[76] Sadly, Bork has it backward. Our Constitution permits majority rule in relatively few areas. In the vast majority of cases, the Framers intended that free individuals would live their lives without government interference.

Fortunately, both the *Lochner* decision and the Fourteenth Amendment are currently enjoying an intellectual renaissance among a new generation of libertarian students and thinkers. As pointed out by Root, "Conservatives and libertarians during their decades in the wilderness papered over profound divisions over one of the most fundamental questions in American law: the role of the courts."[77] Today, that role is still vigorously debated. It's time for libertarians and true conservatives to distinguish between principled judicial engagement in defense of the Constitution and judicial intervention intended to substitute the courts' policy preferences for those of the legislature.

By definition, libertarians (and, in fact, many conservatives) believe in the traditional concept of natural or fundamental rights that should not be overruled by majority rule or executive power, while Borkeans believe in a largely unbridled majoritarianism. The Borkeans rail against "judicial activism" because it often counters majority rule, even if such judicial activism increases rather than diminishes individual liberty.

This disregard for the liberties protected by the Constitution, as properly read, has driven millions of former Republicans, including libertarians, from the ranks of the party. Libertarians, after all, appreciate the great role that courts can and should play in preserving liberty. Again quoting Damon Root, "Libertarians typically favor an aggressive judiciary that is willing to overturn mistaken precedents and strike down unconstitutional state and federal statutes."[78] And that means using the courts to overturn laws that deny gays and lesbians the same rights and privileges that other Americans enjoy.

Robert Levy, chairman of the Cato Institute and a lead attorney in the *District of Columbia v. Heller* Supreme Court gun rights case, agrees. Writing in support of same-sex marriage rights in the *New York Daily News* on January 7, 2010, he argued, "To pass constitutional muster, racial discrimination had to survive 'strict scrutiny' by the courts. Government had to demonstrate a compelling need for its regulations, show they would be effective, and narrowly craft the rules so they didn't sweep more broadly than necessary. That same regime should apply when government discriminates based on gender preference."[79] The fact that this discrimination has existed throughout this country's history does not justify it, let alone render it consistent with our constitutional values. Righting a legal wrong, no matter how deeply ingrained in our society it may be, is still, in the eyes of libertarians, a moral imperative that the courts are constitutionally obligated to undertake.

It is time, therefore, for all libertarians to explicitly reframe this issue and explain to conservatives and Republicans alike the fundamental moral and constitutional principles involved. The courts can and should overturn statutes and constitutional measures that interfere with liberty and equal rights. Libertarians must use their increasing visibility and influence nationwide, particularly within the Republican Party, to support not just economic freedom and a more peaceful foreign policy but also greater personal freedom and legal equality. Contrary to what opponents of gay marriage say about judicial activism, courts, then, do have an important role to play in protecting rights, and most libertarians and many conservatives support that role.

Two federal court cases currently under way highlight this intellectual divide on constitutional rights and could have profound effects on the future of gay marriage in this country.

The first case, *Perry v. Schwarzenegger*, was adjudicated in federal district court in San Francisco. It was a federal constitutional challenge to Proposition 8, the 2008 California statewide initiative that overturned (in a 52–48 percent vote) an earlier state supreme court decision legalizing gay marriage. The case brought together an unlikely duo of lawyers arguing the case for the plaintiffs: well-known conservative attorney and former solicitor general Ted Olson (under President George W. Bush) and David Boies, the Democratic attorney who represented Al Gore in the famous 2001 *Bush v. Gore* Supreme Court case. Ironically, the attorney representing the Bush campaign in that case was Ted Olson.

Olson's excellent conservative credentials, of course, have posed a public relations challenge to the supporters of Proposition 8. In the January 9, 2010, issue of *Newsweek*, he wrote a trenchant essay defending a right to gay marriage in which he bemoaned the fact that "many of my fellow conservatives have an almost knee-jerk hostility toward gay marriage. This does not make sense, because same-sex unions promote the values conservatives prize. . . . The fact that individuals who happen to be gay want to share in this vital social institution is evidence that conservative ideals enjoy widespread acceptance. Conservatives should celebrate this, rather than lament it."[80] When marriage equality becomes the norm in this country, it will be due in no small part to libertarians and conservatives like Ted Olson.

Proposition 8 won its slim majority in part because of the substantial legal protections for gay couples already written into California law, an argument actually used by the proponents of Proposition 8. Supporters of gay marriage, however, argued that equal treatment extends beyond mere legal protection. The state cannot recognize heterosexual unions as "marriages" while refusing to accord that same recognition to gay unions. By stigmatizing gay couples in that manner, said the plaintiffs, Proposition 8 violated the US Constitution's guarantees of due process and equal protection.

Washington, DC, attorney Charles J. Cooper, representing the defenders of Proposition 8, said the state has a vested interest in opposing same-sex marriage. It is "fundamental to the very existence and survival of the human race"[81] that marriage be limited to opposite-sex couples. Cooper never said exactly how gay marriage would lead to the end of procreation by heterosexual couples. He repeated the canard that "the procreation goal is at the heart of marriage," but he could not explain why the state allows millions of heterosexuals to marry who do not or cannot procreate. It seems the case against gay marriage is more about emotional venting against homosexuals than rational argument. Even Cooper himself, when asked by the presiding judge, Vaughn R. Walker, why Proposition 8 backers produced no evidence that same-sex marriage would hurt heterosexual marriage, replied, "I don't know. I don't know."[82]

The two witnesses for the defense were also hard pressed to offer good reasons why gays should be forbidden to marry. One of them, David Blankenhorn, president of the Institute for American Values, lamented the fact that marriage is being weakened by rising divorce and illegitimacy rates. But the *New York Times* pointed out that Blankenhorn "could not convincingly explain what the genders of married couples had to do with that."[83] Ironically, Blankenhorn "acknowledged that marriage is a 'public good' that would benefit same-sex couples and their children, and that to allow same-sex marriage 'would be a victory for the worthy ideas of tolerance and inclusion.'"[84]

On August 5, 2010, Judge Walker handed down his stunning and largely libertarian opinion throwing out Proposition 8, writing that it "fails to advance any rational basis in singling out gay men and lesbians for denial of a marriage license. Indeed, the evidence shows Proposition 8 does nothing more than enshrine . . . the notion that opposite-sex couples are superior to same-sex couples."[85] Judge Walker added that Proposition 8 violates both the Equal Protection and the Due Process clauses of the Fourteenth Amendment. Robert Levy, co-chair of the advisory board to the American Foundation for Equal Rights, which supported overturning Proposition 8, stated that "the judge and this court bravely confronted wrongful discrimination and came down on the right side—defending and enforcing equal protection, as demanded by the Constitution."[86]

Ilya Shapiro, editor of the *Cato Supreme Court Review*, agreed, adding, "This all could have been averted if government just got out of the marriage business entirely: have civil unions for whoever wants them—which would be a contractual basket of rights not unlike business partnerships—and let religious and other private institutions confer whatever sacraments they want. If the state provides the institution of marriage, however, it has to provide it to all people."[87] That statement goes to the heart of Judge Walker's opinion concerning the Equal Protection and Due Process clauses of the Fourteenth Amendment.

Even some conservative newspapers applauded Judge Walker's decision. The *Pittsburgh Tribune-Review* said, "Judge Walker found no legitimate state interest in treating gay and lesbian couples any differently from heterosexual couples. . . . And he's spot on."[88] The *Orange County Register*'s editorial page commended the decision, having stated during the Proposition 8 campaign in 2008 that "guarantees of individual rights are included in constitutions precisely to ensure that such rights cannot be taken away, by majority vote, legislative enactment, or administrative decision. . . . The right to marry is a fundamental individual right that must be provided equally to all people desiring to marry."[89]

More and more conservatives are coming to understand that marriage equality is completely consistent with the traditional libertarian values of limited government and personal freedom.

Nevertheless, supporters of Proposition 8 immediately attacked the opinion (and the judge), often using vicious and extreme language. Chuck Donovan of the Heritage Foundation accused Judge Walker of "judicial tyranny,"[90] and Robert Knight of the Far Right Coral Ridge Ministries called Walker part of "the criminalization of not only Christianity but of the foundational values of civilization itself."[91] Ironically, Judge Walker was first nominated for the bench by President Ronald Reagan on the recommendation of Attorney General Edwin Meese. He was opposed by Senate Democrats, the National Association for the Advancement of Colored People, the Human Rights Campaign Fund, and the American Civil Liberties Union, among other liberal organizations, making the charge that he is some sort of closet liberal rather silly.

And note the utterly over-the-top rhetoric of extremists like Knight, long known for his apocalyptic statements regarding homosexuality. He equates simple legal equality vis-à-vis a government license to "the criminalization" of Christianity. Clearly, legal equality impinges in no way on religious freedom or Christianity. The only thing marriage equality interferes with is the "right" of Knight and his colleagues to force their religious values on the rest of us. He and his fellow culture warriors have turned the meaning of religious freedom on its head.

This case, in fact, demonstrates the intellectual bankruptcy and dishonesty of so many on the right who characterize this issue as an apocalyptic liberal or leftist assault on American values and freedom. In fact, the decision in this case represents just the opposite: an expansion of individual rights forcing the government to treat all its citizens the same way, with special rights for none. When you have a prominent conservative attorney like Ted Olson and a libertarian attorney like Robert Levy both supporting the plaintiffs in their quest for marriage equality, along with a Republican, libertarian-leaning judge deciding the case, you have thrown the usual right-wing clichés about judicial activism and the end of civilization as we know it out the window.

As expected, this decision was appealed to the US Court of Appeals for the Ninth Circuit, which enjoined same-sex marriages from being performed until the case is adjudicated. Because state officials such as the governor and the attorney general refused to appeal Judge Walker's decision, it fell to the California Supreme Court to decide if private parties have standing to pursue an appeal. On November 17, 2011, it declared that supporters of Proposition 8 had standing to continue the appeals process in the Ninth Circuit. The case, now known as *Perry v. Brown*, took another important step forward on February 7, 2012, when the Ninth Circuit Court, not unexpectedly, ruled Proposition 8 unconstitutional, saying it served no purpose "other than to lessen the status and human dignity of gays and lesbians" in California. This decision is being appealed by Proposition 8 supporters, and the case will undoubtedly make it to the US Supreme Court, most likely for the 2012–2013 term.

The other pivotal court case was decided in federal district court in Boston in July 2010. Judge Joseph L. Tauro ruled parts of the 1996 federal Defense of Marriage Act unconstitutional. As discussed in chapter 3, the DOMA legally defines marriage as a union between a man and a woman at the federal level. The law declares that the federal government will recognize only traditional marriage for the purposes of public policy. This denies the growing number of legally wed same-sex couples in this country, now numbering more than one hundred thousand,[92] many economic and legal benefits and privileges automatically granted by the US government to opposite-sex married couples.

Although a lifelong Republican appointed by President Richard Nixon, Judge Tauro ruled that the provision of the law that restricts spousal benefits such as health insurance to married couples violates the right of same-sex couples to equal protection under the law and interferes with the traditional right of states—in this case Massachusetts, where gay marriage is legal—to set their own marriage policies. "The federal government, by enacting and enforcing DOMA, plainly encroaches upon the firmly entrenched province of the state,"[93] the judge wrote. Supporters hailed the ruling because it affirmed the right of same-sex couples to receive the same federal spousal benefits and protections as other married couples. Seven married couples and three widowers from Massachusetts brought the suit, arguing that DOMA violated their constitutional right to equal protection.

Some opponents of same-sex marriage, of course, condemned the ruling and called it "another blatant example of a judge playing legislator," when in fact it exemplifies exactly what judges are supposed to do:

rule on the constitutionality of laws, regardless of whether they are passed by legislatures or the result of popular votes. Not surprisingly, however, some Tea Party conservatives supported the decision because they agreed with the Tenth Amendment jurisprudence on which it was based.[94] This case is now on appeal as well, and it also could go all the way to the Supreme Court.

One thing is sure: whether by court order, legislative approval, or eventual popular vote, same-sex marriage will continue to gain support, as we have seen from the polling discussed earlier in this chapter. Those Republicans who continue to block it (and other forms of relationship recognition like civil unions) will become more and more marginalized, and the Republican Party will lose an entire generation or two of young people who are willing to do what the party currently will not: support the Constitution's promise of liberty and justice for all.

5

THE RISE, FALL, AND RESURRECTION OF THE MODERN CONSERVATIVE MOVEMENT

The growth surge in the libertarian wing of the Republican Party over the past several years has brought to the forefront the long-standing philosophical differences and tensions between libertarians and more traditional conservatives, not just on social issues but also on a wide range of topics, including foreign policy, judicial activism and the role of the courts, and even the fundamental bread-and-butter economic issues that supposedly unite all conservatives. Many conservatives today talk about what they call the three-legged stool of modern conservatism, referring to the three basic kinds of modern conservative: economic, social, and national defense conservatives. In reality, however, these three legs are not just simply areas of emphasis or focus: in many cases, they represent a deep philosophical divide within the broader movement over fundamental questions like the proper role of government, the extent of individual rights, and even what constitutes "national defense."

We have seen these differences reflected in the field of Republican presidential contenders, representing a range of positions on issues such as gay rights and foreign military intervention. Ron Paul, Jon Huntsman, and Gary Johnson for the most part promoted a more libertarian agenda versus the hard Right positions of Michele Bachmann, Rick Perry, Newt Gingrich, Herman Cain, Rick Santorum, and Mitt Romney.

In the modern era, this tension goes back at least to the 1950s, when the various strands of American conservatism were sorting themselves out in a new postwar world. It boiled over in the 1970s, when the modern libertarian movement exploded onto the American political scene as a separate and distinct part of the wider conservative movement, with its own set of intellectuals and writers, political activists, economists, and Nobel laureates—even its own political party.

A brief history of the modern conservative movement, then—including that of one of its dominant strains, libertarianism—will demonstrate how it sprang intellectually from its philosophical forebear, classical liberalism. This history will show that the intellectual and cultural tensions and differences that exist today within the conservative movement are nothing new and explain why they are not as minor as many conservatives, and even some libertarians, would like to believe. So let's start at the beginning.

WHAT WAS CLASSICAL LIBERALISM?

Wikipedia defines classical liberalism as follows: "A philosophy committed to the ideal of limited government, constitutionalism, the rule of law, due process, and liberty of individuals, including freedom of religion, speech, press, assembly, and free markets."[1]

If you think this description sounds much like the philosophy of modern conservatism, particularly libertarianism, you're right, but what we today call classical liberalism (to distinguish it from modern liberalism) was also the fundamental philosophy of our Founding Fathers and their philosophical soulmates in Europe. It embodied the beliefs and principles we take for granted today as the proper way to organize society. These were the same beliefs and principles that inspired our Founders to write the Declaration of Independence and upon which our Constitution is based.

In the seventeenth, eighteenth, and early nineteenth centuries, however, the freedom-based tenets of classical liberalism were for the most part a completely new way of thinking about the relationship between citizens and their government. The idea that citizens had rights, that they were sovereign and free, or at least should be, represented a radical break with the age-old traditions of the divine right of kings and church theocracy, in which any rights flowed from the monarch, pope, or feudal warlord.

Eighteenth-century political philosophers like John Locke, Adam Smith, and John Stuart Mill[2] laid the intellectual groundwork for the ideas and principles the Founders used to build the new country called the United States by introducing a new political paradigm: the belief that "all men are created equal; that they are endowed by their Creator with certain unalienable rights, that among these are life, liberty, and the pursuit of happiness."[3] Our Founding Fathers were convinced "that to insure these rights, governments are instituted among men, deriving their just powers from the consent of the governed,"[4] and their convictions about the proper way to govern stemmed directly from these philosophers and their intellectual compatriots.

For the first time in human history, the individual became the basic building block of society, and government was now viewed primarily as a means to protect individual rights rather than as a collective body that supersedes them. Citizens were free to pursue their own ends rather than being merely the means to a government-chosen end. Consequently, government had a very limited role. Adam Smith, author of the seminal book *The Wealth of Nations*,[5] for example, outlined just three primary functions of government: protection from foreign invaders, protection of individuals from wrongs committed by other individuals, and building and maintaining what is today called infrastructure—things like roads, bridges, canals, and other public amenities and services.

Classical liberals like Smith espoused the then new ideas of limited government and freedom of individuals against the traditional aristocratic regimes that ruled most of the so-called civilized world—kings, queens, and other "nobility" with few limits on their arbitrary power.

THE PROGRESSIVE ERA AND NEW DEAL

The free market and limited government principles our Founding Fathers built this country on served us well for the next hundred years or so. Federal power ebbed and flowed during this period, especially during times of war, but for the most part, the federal government was small and relatively weak, especially by today's standards.

The post–Civil War era, however, saw a substantial increase in the power and scope of the federal government, particularly in its regulation of business and markets. According to leftist historian Sidney Fine, big business during this period sought and got "a national banking system, a high protective tariff, generous land grants to railway corporations,"[6] and other benefits from government intervention. Classical liberal historian Arthur Ekirch writes, "Instead of the limited state desired by Jeffersonian believers in an agrarian society, the post–Civil War era was characterized by the passage of a stream of tariffs, taxes, and subsidies all unprecedented in the their volume and scope."[7]

During this period, both major parties were undergoing ideological changes, and both had classical liberal (or free market) factions, as well as more populist, pro–big government, elements. President Grover Cleveland, for example, a free market Democrat who supported a gold standard and opposed tariffs and US military adventures abroad, won two nonconsecutive terms, from 1885 to 1889 and 1893 to 1897. Within his own party, he battled populists like William Jennings Bryan, who represented the anti–big business, agrarian wing of his party, as well as segregationists and prohibitionists.

The Republicans were splitting along ideological lines as well. William McKinley opposed the antiliberal populist policies of Bryan and was twice elected president over him, but the Republican Party also had its "progressive" wing, which would soon have more in common philosophically with Bryan than with President McKinley and other classical liberals. This new wing of the party was represented by people like President Teddy Roosevelt, who eventually broke with the Republican Party and formed his own Bull Moose Party in 1912, as well as many members of Congress from the Northeast, such as Senator John Sherman (author of the Sherman Antitrust Act) and Senate Republican leader Nelson Aldrich of Rhode Island, who successfully introduced the bill to establish the nation's first income tax in 1902.

This radical new political movement, called Progressivism, was now thoroughly entrenched in both major political parties and represented a sharp break with the political philosophy of the Founding Fathers. Its partisans exhibited an almost unquenchable faith in government planning and rule by experts that rapidly supplanted our traditional beliefs in limited government and the primacy of the individual.

These sweeping philosophical changes were perhaps best symbolized by a Progressive journalist named Herbert Croly, the single most influential promoter of Progressive thought of his time. His 1909 book *The Promise of American Life*[8] excoriated the conventional wisdom that

America's traditional values of individual liberty and free enterprise were best suited to build and maintain prosperity. As libertarian political scientist John Samples wrote in *The Struggle to Limit Government*,[9] "Croly recoiled from what he saw as the rampant individualism and purified selfishness fostered by Jeffersonian ideals. Jeffersonian liberty did not lead to the correct pattern of economic outcomes."[10] Croly argued that "the traditional American confidence in individual freedom has resulted in a morally and socially undesirable distribution of wealth."[11]

Consequently, he proposed, and the Progressive movement successfully campaigned for, a whole host of government controls over the economy and welfare programs designed to mitigate that "undesirable distribution of wealth." Many Progressives of that era were often motivated by strongly held religious beliefs and thought it the proper duty of the state to promote those religious beliefs through government programs to aid the poor and disenfranchised. The free market, they thought, often left men to fend for themselves without the security of government aid and welfare. Progressives believed man could be molded and perfected to act in certain ways. The national disaster of Prohibition, for example, was one outcome of this new union of religious activism and political power. Many Progressives also supported eugenics, a popular movement holding that certain races and social groups exhibited characteristics and lifestyles harmful to the greater public good and should be inhibited from reproducing. Today's merging of political activism and religion is clearly nothing new in American history; it has been going on for as long as this country has been in existence, toward a variety of ends.

THE GOLDEN AGE OF CAPITALISM

The Progressive movement's growth receded somewhat with the end of World War I and the widespread prosperity of the 1920s, seen by many as a golden age of sorts for American capitalism and the widespread distribution of material goods to the average person that it accomplishes so well. The meaning of liberalism was rapidly changing; those who espoused the once "liberal" ideas of limited government and free markets were more often now labeled "conservative." Historian Garland Tucker, in fact, said the 1924 presidential election marked the "high tide of American conservatism,"[12] since both major party candidates campaigned on platforms of smaller government and tax cuts. President Calvin Coolidge won the election, and the economy boomed for the rest of the decade.

The stock market crash of 1929, however, led to government policies that soon ended that widespread prosperity. Although the economy and employment actually recovered rather quickly following the crash (the unemployment rate was only 6.5 percent one year later[13]), the statist policies and programs instituted by President Herbert Hoover (himself a "progressive" Republican) to address the lingering problems, along with a severe monetary contraction engineered by the Federal Reserve and the passage of the Smoot-Hawley tariffs, plunged the nation into the Great Depression, from which it never fully recovered until the end of World War II. Governor Franklin Delano Roosevelt of New York, who campaigned as a conservative who would cut federal spending by 25 percent, was elected in a landslide in 1932.

Although true conservatives throughout this period loudly and vigorously opposed and criticized President Roosevelt's New Deal policies of widespread federal intervention into the economy, they were mostly ineffective in stopping or curbing them until the late 1930s, when a coalition of congressional Republicans and conservative Democrats finally put an end to Roosevelt's ability to implement his programs and policies. But by then, the federal government had reached new heights in control over the economy and levels of spending rarely seen up to that point. Unfortunately, many "modern" Republicans of the day, including Thomas Dewey, who twice challenged President Roosevelt, had little interest in challenging the philosophical basis of the New Deal, and most of the Republican Party establishment agreed with him.

Not until the end of World War II was there a revival of sorts of a movement based on the classical liberal ideals of limited government, one with the aim of rolling back at least some of the New Deal programs. By this time, however, the evolution of American liberalism into something very different from its original, classical form was complete. In the words of historian William J. Novak, by 1937 liberalism had gone "from laissez-faire constitutionalism to New Deal statism, from classical liberalism to democratic social-welfarism."[14] In short, those who had been called liberals in the eighteenth and early nineteenth centuries were now called conservatives, and liberals were now the advocates of greater government power over individuals and the economy that we know today.

POSTWAR CONSERVATISM

The conservative movement as we know it began to take shape in the postwar period. It was a broad coalition of traditional economic conservatives, a feisty if dwindling libertarian movement of Old Right politicians and intellectuals, and a newer kind of conservative intellectual, often Catholic, who was interested more in the traditional morality and culture of Western civilization than economics. While this coalition was united in its hatred of communism and socialism, it included a wide range of often conflicting views not just on foreign policy but also on economic issues and the role of the state in peoples' lives. An overview of these three basic factions of the conservative movement shows a remarkable similarity to the division and disagreements in the conservative movement today, divisions that are not likely to be easily overcome.

The newest additions to the postwar conservative movement were intellectuals like Russell Kirk, author of *The Conservative Mind*,[15] who believed that American conservatives placed too much emphasis on the traditional economic issues that Republicans had long focused on. Kirk's was more a philosophy of fidelity to a European-style conservatism of rule by elites based on religion, divine revelation, and a devotion to existing social traditions and customs. Historian Gerald J. Russello listed six basic canons of Kirk's philosophy:[16]

- A belief in a transcendent order, which Kirk described variously as based in tradition, divine revelation, or natural law
- An affection for the "variety and mystery" of human existence
- A conviction that society requires orders and classes that emphasize "natural" distinctions
- A belief that property and freedom are closely linked
- A faith in custom, convention, and prescription

- A recognition that innovation must be tied to existing traditions and customs, which entails a respect for the political value of prudence

Not surprisingly, Kirk was extremely hostile to libertarianism, with its emphasis on individual rights and secular nature. He actually wrote that the Declaration of Independence "was not conspicuously American in its ideas or its phrases, and not even characteristically Jeffersonian."[17] He despised the Enlightenment, the eighteenth-century philosophical movement that had been such a profound inspiration for most of our Founding Fathers, including Thomas Jefferson.[18] Even though in his core beliefs Kirk had virtually nothing in common with the economic conservatives and libertarians of his time, he and his intellectual brethren were nonetheless part of the conservative coalition, much like the Far Right theocrats in today's conservative movement who openly despise libertarianism because of its secular nature and emphasis on individual rights rather than religion and government's alleged role in promoting it.

Other traditionalists and Catholic intellectuals, such as James Burnham, Willmore Kendall, and L. Brent Bozell, became popular as well, and they would later join Kirk in taking up residence in 1955 at a new magazine launched by William F. Buckley, a then up-and-coming conservative intellectual who made an entire career out of tweaking the liberal establishment, as well as other factions in the larger conservative movement. Buckley and the magazine, *National Review*, eventually became icons of the conservative movement, and the magazine remains an influential organ in the movement to this day.

But the philosophical differences between conservatives and libertarians grew, even as some attempted to bridge the intellectual gap between them. One was Frank Meyer, who co-founded *National Review* with Buckley and was also an ex-communist (like most of the magazine's early writers). Meyer coined the term "fusionism"[19] to refer to a political philosophy that attempted to bridge the two primary schools of conservative thought by emphasizing their common intellectual elements of support for free markets, fealty to the US Constitution, and limited government, although even the definition of the latter was a matter of dispute.

Ultimately, however, many tradition-bound conservatives could not overcome the fact that their first allegiance was to their private religious and cultural values rather than the classical liberal principles upon which the modern conservative movement was supposedly based. The conservative/libertarian alliance was an uneasy one, particularly with the racism and homophobia that was often rampant among conservatives.

A 1957 editorial in *National Review*, for example, opined, "The central question that emerges . . . is whether the White community in the South is entitled to take such measures as are necessary to prevail, politically and culturally, in areas in which it does not predominate numerically? The sobering answer is Yes—the White community is so entitled because, for the time being, it is the advanced race."[20] Although the editors of *National Review* today must cringe at such words, the fact is that most conservatives in the 1950s were indifferent to or supportive of Jim Crow laws and segregation.

Conservatives and Republicans in general had little or no sympathy for the rights of gay Americans as well. President Dwight D. Eisenhower, for example, instituted a ban on gays and lesbians working for any government agency,[21] and congressional committees, Democrats as well as Republicans, routinely organized witch hunts against homosexuals who might be present somewhere in the federal government,[22] all without a peep of protest from any conservative or Republican leader in Congress. It was a sorry time in American history for all minorities. A more detailed overview of gay rights in the 1950s and 1960s is presented in chapter 1.

A leading intellectual light at the other end of the conservative spectrum from the traditionalists centered at *National Review* was the free market icon and Austrian economist Friedrich Hayek. Hayek's most famous work was *The Road to Serfdom*,[23] published in 1944. One of the most influential economic works of the twentieth century, it has sold over two million copies. In it, he "warned of the danger of tyranny that inevitably results from government control of economic decision-making through central planning."[24] Hayek was as critical of the fascist regimes against which we had gone to war as he was of the socialist ones that would emerge as our new adversaries. He argued that they shared the common thread of government control and direction of the economy, and he made the case that civil liberties were an essential part of a free market.

In 1945, an abridged version of his book was published in the popular *Reader's Digest* magazine, where it reached millions of ordinary

Americans with the conservative message of free markets and limited government.[25] Fortunately, *The Road to Serfdom* is experiencing something of a revival today with the newfound prominence of the Tea Party movement.

Perhaps the most famous conservative politician of this era was Senator Robert A. Taft from Ohio, who combined the traditional free market values of classical liberals with a strident belief in an anti-interventionist foreign policy, a belief that characterized much of the conservative Republican movement after World War II, including not only members of the Old Right who had opposed Roosevelt and the New Deal but also conservative Democrats, many of whom had opposed parts of the New Deal as well as US intervention in World War II.[26] All of them had become part of a broad postwar movement against foreign military intervention, including in the Korean War. Even conservative Catholics like Russell Kirk were part of this opposition to the war, as were many House Republicans, who became the majority in the 1948 congressional election.

This right-wing antiwar coalition did not last long in the face of America's rapidly growing fear of communism, however. By the time Senator Taft died in 1953, after having lost the Republican presidential nomination to General Dwight D. Eisenhower, a Dewey-style Republican, most of the conservative Right was now firmly in the interventionist camp. Although the broader conservative movement included a noisy remnant of intellectuals and activists still steeped in the anti-interventionist philosophy of the Old Right, anti-communism and its corollary, an activist foreign policy, ruled the day. Communism, not the federal government, was Public Enemy No. 1.

Most conservatives today, in fact, are not even aware of this heritage of antiwar activism by much of the conservative Right during that period, although those antiwar beliefs are enjoying a renaissance with the increasing visibility of Ron Paul and his followers within the Republican Party.

Throughout the next decade, an intellectual orthodoxy in the conservative movement developed in both domestic and foreign affairs, led in large part by William F. Buckley and his somewhat eclectic group of New Right intellectuals and free market economists at *National Review*.

Many libertarians were declared persona non grata by Buckley and his crowd, including the popular novelist and philosopher Ayn Rand, whose 1,168-page 1957 novel *Atlas Shrugged*[27] sparked a following of millions of readers for her novels, if not her philosophy of objectivism, which combined a fierce belief in laissez-faire capitalism with an equally fierce belief in atheism, opposition to altruism, and freedom from religion. Broadly speaking, the conservative movement now included factions and strains that had as many disagreements with each other as they did with those on the left.[28]

Moderate Republicans like President Eisenhower and his vice president, Richard Nixon, ruled the Republican establishment for the entire decade, but Nixon was no match for the charming Senator Jack Kennedy from Massachusetts, who narrowly defeated Nixon in 1960 (apparently with the help of a few friends like Chicago mayor Richard Daley).

MR. CONSERVATIVE

The presidential candidacy of Senator Barry Goldwater in 1964 brought together most of the disparate elements of the small and somewhat dormant conservative movement and energized them in a way not seen since Robert Taft's run for the presidency in 1952, especially since most conservatives reviled the moderate Republicans who ruled their party, elected officials like Governor Nelson Rockefeller of New York, who ran against Goldwater for the Republican nomination for president. Although some hard-core libertarians like economist Murray Rothbard and his followers hated Goldwater for his strident anti-communist foreign policy, most libertarians took heart in his relatively radical political program, outlined in his book *Conscience of a Conservative*,[29] released in 1962.

Goldwater's book and campaign energized a whole new generation of conservative and libertarian activists and laid the foundation for a growing conservative movement, even in the wake of Goldwater's historic defeat by Lyndon Johnson. The Goldwater campaign also launched the career of another famous conservative icon, an actor named Ronald

Reagan, who made a short film in 1964 called *A Time for Choosing* extolling the virtues of Goldwater's candidacy. It seemingly helped Reagan more than it did Goldwater, who lost in a landslide.

By the late 1960s, however, the grassroots conservative movement was stronger than ever, and it contained a large contingent of increasingly radical libertarians. Elected in 1966, Ronald Reagan was now the popular governor of California, and conservatives were becoming not only the base of the Republican Party but also part of the political mainstream. The Vietnam War and the growing counterculture of drugs, personal freedom, and gay rights were radicalizing many conservative students as well as those on the left, however, and the philosophical differences between libertarian and conservative activists were as great as ever.

Nowhere was this more evident than in an organization called Young Americans for Freedom (YAF), a Bill Buckley–spawned, nationwide campus organization of conservatives founded in 1960 that had became a battleground between libertarians and "trads," or those who believed in traditional morality, social mores, and gung-ho military intervention, not just in Vietnam but also across the globe. This clash came to a head at the 1969 national convention of YAF in St. Louis, with fights breaking out between antiwar, pro-freedom libertarians and traditionalists who demonstrated with signs and shouts in favor of the war and against "lazy fairies," a sarcastic reference to the laissez-faire beliefs of libertarians that also illustrates that the overt bigotry of many social conservatives in today's movement is not a new thing.

Though not a movement conservative or one who held core conservative beliefs, former vice president Richard Nixon was considered the conservative candidate in the 1968 presidential election (not a difficult thing when running against Vice President Hubert H. Humphrey, an enthusiastic supporter of big government), and he won the election in a three-way race that included populist conservative and former segregationist governor of Alabama George Wallace.

Real conservatives soon realized that Richard Nixon was anything but. He initiated many big government, Great Society–like programs and policies, from new antipoverty and affirmative action programs to the creation of the Environmental Protection Agency. And Nixon's imposition of wage and price controls in 1971 simply confirmed the suspicions that nearly every conservative and libertarian harbored about him.

The Vietnam War raged on during his first term, and the countercultural social movements—from civil rights to gay rights to widespread use of illegal drugs like marijuana—continued to grow. Libertarians were often on the counterculture's side of the barricade on these issues.[30] There was also, however, a backlash of sorts against the rapid cultural change and political dissent sweeping the nation, and when presented with a choice between left-liberal Senator George McGovern, the antiwar candidate, and President Nixon, Americans went in a big way for Nixon, who won in a landslide in 1972.

But within two years, Nixon's presidency had unraveled under the Watergate scandal, and he resigned in 1974, with Gerald Ford, his moderate, mainstream vice president, becoming president. Ford was a likeable man, but conservatives viewed him as a "me-too" Republican, a derogatory term for Republicans who didn't want to rock the boat in Washington politics by actively opposing big government.

While the establishment Republicans ruled in Washington, DC, the conservative movement continued to grow, especially the movement's infrastructure. The Heritage Foundation was founded in 1973, and the Cato Institute, its more libertarian cousin, began in 1977. Libertarian ideas continued to grow in popularity as well. In 1971, the Libertarian Party was founded by libertarians disenchanted with Richard Nixon and the recent record of the Republican Party, and it achieved notable visibility and some electoral success, particularly in its early years in states like California. In that same year, William F. Buckley verbally excommunicated libertarians for a second time from "his" conservative movement, and tensions between the two factions hardened.

The intellectual renaissance of libertarian philosophy continued, however, with the 1974 publication of Robert Nozick's *Anarchy, State, and Utopia*,[31] which won the National Book Award the following year. Libertarian and conservative economic theories also grew in popularity among intellectuals and the public, with Friedrich Hayek winning the Nobel Prize in economics in 1974 and Milton Friedman, perhaps the best-known free market economist of the second half of the twentieth century, winning the prize in 1976. Libertarianism had become the avant-garde of the conservative movement, once considered the province of stodgy old white men. Governor Reagan, who challenged President Ford for the Republican nomination in 1976, became the titular head of the conservative movement when his second term as governor came to an end in 1975.

What would become the most divisive and unpopular Supreme Court decision of the twentieth century was issued in 1973 in the case of *Roe v. Wade*. The ruling legalized most cases of abortion, previously an issue handled by the states. Ironically, the decision was not initially unpopular with evangelicals. In 1971 and 1974, for example, Southern Baptists supported legislation that would have eased state restrictions on abortion, including in cases of rape, incest, and severe fetal deformity or to protect the emotional and physical health of the mother.[32] By the time Reagan was elected in 1980, however, there was almost universal opposition to the decision by those on the right, although most libertarians supported the Court's decision because of the increased role it gave to individual choice and conscience. Today, *Roe v. Wade* is a litmus test for nearly all Republican candidates.

Federal policy changes, however, reflected little of the conservative and libertarian intellectual ferment the country was experiencing in the 1970s. After an unremarkable term of just two years, and with the country mired in recession, President Ford lost the 1976 election and was replaced by evangelical Georgia governor Jimmy Carter. Far more interested in their religious beliefs than free market economics and political philosophy, most self-described Christian evangelicals supported Governor Carter, and the nation descended into a dismal four years of economic stagnation and turmoil. The country was ripe for a big change.

THE FAILED RESURRECTION

That change came in 1980 with the election of Ronald Reagan as president, a seminal moment for conservatives and libertarians alike, who had high hopes for a national candidate who had explicitly labeled himself a libertarian. In a 1975 interview with libertarian *Reason* magazine, Reagan had said, "If you analyze it, I believe the very heart and soul of conservatism is libertarianism. . . . The basis of conservatism is a desire for less government interference or less centralized authority or more individual freedom, and this is a pretty general description also of what libertarianism is."[33]

And yet, by the end of his presidency, Reagan had had no more success in reducing the total size or cost of the federal government than he did with state government while governor of California, where spending had gone from $5.7 billion to $10.8 billion during his two terms.[34] While domestic federal discretionary spending dipped some during his first year as president, it rose rapidly thereafter, as did military spending, which nearly doubled during his first term in office.

Although Reagan cut taxes significantly during his first year, his spending cuts did not come close to matching them, so his administration incurred large budget deficits throughout most of his time in office. The national debt doubled, rising from $907 billion in 1980 to $2.6 trillion in 1988.[35] Although the basic tenet of the "supply-side" economic theory that guided his administration—that cutting tax rates would actually result in higher levels of revenue—proved true, at least in the case of high-income earners, its lack of concern about spending cuts and deficits ultimately tarnished its image among economists and the public. Libertarian Republicans and others had a field day in pointing out Reagan's deficiencies on these issues.

After the Democratic Congress denied his initial, fairly large spending cuts, for example, he simply gave up on them. He also passed up opportunities in 1985 for major entitlement reform when his Social Security commission, headed by Alan Greenspan, recommended changes to the program to improve its long-term solvency. Rather than recommend substantive reforms to correct the program's long-term actuarial imbalance, the commission tinkered around the edges and kicked the can down the road. The result is the impending bankruptcy of the program we now face.

Reagan also embarked on a huge defense spending binge. Most conservatives heartily supported it, as did some Democrats, and they credit the buildup with the fall of communism in 1989 during the administration of President George H. W. Bush. Again, however, libertarians and others disagreed, arguing that the fall of the Soviet Union was primarily a result of the internal contradictions of socialism and its inability to produce, and they questioned many of the missions US forces were sent on, from the occupation of Lebanon to the invasion of Granada. In any event, the fall of communism finally melted the glue that had held together the disparate groups and beliefs that comprised the conservative coalition for nearly forty-five years. This ultimately meant that sharper divisions between the various factions would emerge.

Religious Right voters were a strong part of the Reagan coalition, and by the end of Reagan's second term, a plurality of evangelicals had completed the journey from the Democratic to the Republican Party,[36] spurred in large part by Reagan's opposition to abortion and the *Roe v. Wade* Supreme Court decision, which galvanized the Right like no other before or after. But the evangelicals' newfound allegiance to the Republican Party would also have many negative consequences, including the loss of millions of other voters repulsed by their repeated attempts to inject their religious beliefs into public policy. The many hateful comments made by Religious Right leaders like Pat Robertson and Jerry Falwell about AIDS victims and other minorities will forever be a stain on their legacy, and as even a brief review of the websites of the main Religious Right organizations will show, their hatred of gay people persists to this day.

Policy-wise, perhaps the best thing that can be said for Reagan's time in office is that federal spending increased less than it would have under other presidents, and most Americans received a tax cut. But that is a disappointing legacy for a president whom millions of conservatives and libertarians had pinned their hopes on to roll back at least some of the Great Society programs. They had learned that actually reducing the size and scope of government in the face of the many institutional barriers to such cuts would require far more than lip service and a genial personality.

CONTRACT WITH AMERICA

By the time President Bill Clinton was elected, the Religious Right's agenda had become, in the words of conservative columnist William Safire, "God, guns, and gays."[37] Though a bit hyperbolic, of course, the remark is not that far off. As the country witnessed, the new president bit off more than he could chew with his proposal to end the gay ban in the US armed forces and allow gays to serve openly. The proposal, poorly planned and promoted, caused a firestorm. The resulting compromise was the Don't Ask, Don't Tell policy, which supposedly would allow gays to serve if they stayed in the closet. The policy, not surprisingly, led to witch hunts, reprisals, and the discharge of thousands of gay service members. The issue also gave some on the right an excellent platform from which to spew their anti-gay hate.

The next major opportunity for conservatives as well as the Religious Right came with the congressional elections of 1994, when Republicans gained majorities in both the House of Representatives and the Senate for the first time since 1953. Republican voters and independents were highly motivated, much like they were in 2010, by the heavy-handed attempts at federal gun control and national health care by President Clinton, elected in 1992 with just 43 percent of the vote in a three-way race. America was by now a center-right nation, and it had decided that Washington, DC, needed more balance.

Conservative activists, congressional leaders, and even many libertarians were heady with calls for abolition of at least several cabinet-level departments, and in response to the Republican takeover, President Clinton himself declared in his 1995 State of the Union address that "the era of big government is over." If only it were that easy.

The first piece of business tackled by the new Congress was implementation of the provisions of the "Contract with America," the campaign document calling for a combination of procedural and substantive government reforms and spending cuts issued by the House Republicans prior to the election. Parts of the contract were passed in the House, only to be ignored by the Senate or modified by President Clinton. In the end, most of the ninety-five major programs the contract had promised to eliminate survived, but as George Mason University law professor David Bernstein pointed out, the contract "showed that Congress took federalism and limited national government seriously."[38]

Once again, however, the Republican leadership was ill prepared to do political battle with Washington's status quo. It lost the 1995 public relations war precipitated by the Republican Congress's attempt to implement some of its policy agenda and spending cuts by shutting down the federal government, leading to a showdown with the president. President Clinton rebounded from the Democrats' congressional losses and won reelection in 1996, albeit with just 49 percent of the vote.

While a majority of Christian Right voters were active in the Republican Party during the Clinton administration, President Clinton himself sought their votes as well. He actually ran radio commercials on religious stations during the 1996 campaign[39] extolling his support for their values and the fact that he had instituted the Don't Ask, Don't Tell policy for our armed forces. And in 1998, he signed the Defense of Marriage Act, designed to forbid any recognition of the rights of same-sex couples anywhere in the federal government. Support for gay rights among voters had grown during the 1990s, but most legislative victories were still out of reach.

THE BUSH YEARS

George W. Bush's two terms represented perhaps the zenith of Religious Right influence on a president, which is not surprising for such an overtly religious one. Bush considered himself "born-again," and his advisers, particularly longtime aide Karl Rove, were determined to maximize the benefits of that, especially since four million evangelicals had stayed home on Election Day in 2000, leading to the disastrous post-election court battles that eventually put Bush in office even though he actually received slightly fewer votes than Vice President Al Gore. The political capital and goodwill that Bush earned from his leadership after 9/11 didn't last long, and the country soon returned to intensely partisan fighting over abortion rights and funding and President Bush's faith-based initiatives, as well as gay-related issues.

The 2003 Massachusetts Supreme Court decision legalizing gay marriage in that state galvanized the social conservative movement like nothing else since *Roe v. Wade*. The decision in *Goodridge v. Department of Public Health* sent shockwaves throughout the entire country, in fact, not just the conservative movement. Many conservatives, especially religious ones, saw the decision as an attack on Western civilization itself, and they worked feverishly to put as many anti–gay marriage amendments on state ballots as possible during the 2004 election in an effort to prevent other states from legalizing same-sex marriage.

Karl Rove used those state ballot fights to the best of the White House's ability to maximize conservative turnout in those states for Bush's reelection in 2004. Although Bush won a narrow victory (and the amendments all won handily), political experts still differ on the question of how big a role those amendments played in his victory.[40]

What is clear, however, is that Bush's increasing identification with the Religious Right and its causes continued the trend of female, suburban, younger, and independent voters leaving the Republican Party. Libertarians were among those deserting Bush in 2004, as much for his record of massive spending increases and deficits as for his policies of social intolerance and kowtowing to the demands of the Religious Right.

Two issues in particular during President Bush's second term personified the shift that had taken place in the Republican Party over the past few decades with regard to social issues. One was the Federal Marriage Amendment, a top priority for social conservatives despite its obvious clash with the longtime conservative belief in federalism, the constitutional principle that the individual states should handle those matters not expressly given to the federal government.

Many conservatives proposed amending the Constitution to specifically outlaw same-sex marriage anywhere in the country. Various forms of such an amendment were introduced in Congress both before and after the 2004 election, but the issue took on greater urgency after Bush's reelection. Supporters knew they would have a relatively small window of opportunity to get the amendment through both houses of Congress.

Although President Bush reportedly supported a version of the amendment that would have allowed states the right to implement "civil unions" instead of same-sex marriage, the versions that were introduced would have effectively outlawed any kind of relationship recognition for gay couples. Fortunately, the amendment finally died in 2006 when it failed to win cloture in either the House or the Senate—that is, the vote totals necessary to cut off debate and actually conduct an up or down vote on the amendment itself. That same year, Republicans lost control of both the House and the Senate, and the Federal Marriage Amendment has mostly been a dead issue since then.

The other issue that galvanized the Religious Right—and subsequently generated a backlash of disgust with it—involved the infamous case of Terri Schiavo in 2005.[41] Schiavo was a wife and mother who had suffered massive brain damage after experiencing cardiac arrest in 1990. In 1998, her husband, Michael Schiavo, petitioned the courts to allow him to remove her feeding tube after she had spent eight years in a vegetative state, an option he had under Florida law. Unfortunately, her parents and other family members disagreed, and a long and contentious court battle began between them and her husband. Although her doctors pronounced her in a "persistent vegetative state," pro-life groups and politicians began to intervene, filing case after case to prevent the husband's wishes from being followed.

When the state courts sided with Schiavo, the Florida legislature and Governor Jeb Bush intervened by passing a law giving them jurisdiction to make the decision about whether to remove the feeding tube, a radical intervention into what was—and should be—a family matter. When the courts again sided with the husband, Republicans in Congress called him to testify before Congress and soon thereafter passed a law overruling many years' worth of state court decisions that favored Schiavo by shifting the case to federal courts. President Bush flew back to Washington from his ranch in Crawford, Texas, specifically to sign the bill. Religious Right and pro-life groups were ecstatic over this unprecedented federal intervention into a private matter that would have been unthinkable just a few years prior.

Federal courts (including the US Supreme Court), however, also ruled in favor of the husband's prerogative to remove the feeding tube. On March 18, 2005, Terri Schiavo's feeding tube was removed for the final time, and she passed away, thus ending seven years of court battles. The sight of mostly Republican senators and congressmen preening before television cameras, commenting about such a personal and painful decision, was unseemly, and for millions of Americans, the Schiavo case emblematized the Religious Right's overweening interference into the private lives of those who don't share its religious values.

As we have seen regarding so many other issues of personal and religious freedom, including gay rights, the Religious Right was on the wrong side of public opinion about the Schiavo case. A CNN poll conducted from March 18 to 20, 2005, showed that a significant majority of Americans agreed with the courts' decision to allow the removal of Schiavo's feeding tube, including 54 percent of both Republicans and independents.[42] ABC News polling that same month showed 63 percent of the public supported removal of the tube, versus 28 percent opposed,[43] with 70 percent calling it "inappropriate" for Congress to have involved itself in the controversy. Even 54 percent of conservatives in this poll supported removal of the tube, while evangelicals were evenly divided: 46 percent were in favor, and 44 percent were opposed.[44] Clearly, the right-wing groups that made this a cause célèbre for their fund-raising did not represent even a majority of the evangelical community, let alone the public at large. After this sordid event ended, the image of the Republican leadership as firmly under the thumb of the Religious Right was cemented in the public's mind, and the electoral consequences of that perception became very clear when Republicans lost both houses of Congress in 2006.

Unfortunately, strident opposition to gay rights and other issues of personal freedom—not to mention a record of fiscal irresponsibility and profligate spending—will always be part of the Bush administration's legacy. While libertarians and some conservatives realized early on in the Bush administration the true nature of its policies, most conservatives were either co-opted by or complicit in them. As a consequence, the basic principles of free enterprise, limited government, and individual liberty were sullied by the very people who should have championed them.

OBAMA AND THE BIRTH OF TEA PARTY NATION

The unpopularity of President Bush, on top of the Great Recession of 2008, when the stock market nosedived just before the election, sealed the deal for the Democrats and Senator Barack Obama in the 2008 election. They were swept into power among talk of a new kind of politics in Washington, DC. Although Obama was arguably one of the most radical presidential candidates in many years, dislike and distrust of Senator John McCain for his history of off-the-reservation policy positions dampened the support and enthusiasm of many conservatives for the Republican ticket, despite his oddball choice of running mate in Alaska governor Sarah Palin, who quickly became the darling of the social conservative Right. However, conservative grassroots support and enthusiasm for Palin was no match for the loss of independents, moderates, and younger voters to Obama, who won with almost 53 percent of the vote to McCain's 46 percent. Even 20 percent of conservatives voted for Obama.[45] Democrats also increased their numbers in both houses of Congress, with large majorities in both. It looked like the Republican Party was headed into the wilderness for a very long time.

Obama's honeymoon did not last long, however. While hard-core conservative activists never had any doubt about what they saw as Obama's radical views and philosophy about government, his proposed health-care reforms, ironically called the Patient Protection and Affordable Care Act, created widespread anger and a backlash even outside the conservative movement not seen since President Clinton attempted to push through his health-care bill in the early 1990s. Obama's $1 trillion proposal and its draconian rules and regulations would spell the end of health care as we know it, warned conservatives and libertarians alike. An enormous grassroots movement of millions of Americans actively opposed the bill and challenged its socialistic premises in rallies and town hall meetings around the country. Although they came close to killing it, the bill was signed into law on March 25, 2010. Many conservatives were waking up to the fact that a lot of the time, effort, and money spent on social issues would have been better spent preparing for the epic fight over health care and the other fiscal and economic issues the country suddenly faced.

The president's budget-busting spending proposals and $1 trillion stimulus bill, on top of his health-care "reforms," proved too much for many Americans. The Tea Party burst onto the political scene in 2009 and quickly became a household name. Although the movement actually began in 2008 under President Bush, especially after Congress passed his Troubled Asset Relief Program bill and other proposals to deal with the collapse of the housing market, it really took off under President Obama. After a decade of focusing on social issues, particularly gay marriage and other gay rights–related issues, conservatives finally began to focus like a laser beam on economic issues and the damage Obama's proposals would do to the country. And the movement was remarkably successful in a short period in building a broad coalition of opposition to the Democrats' agenda.

In November 2009, in two closely watched state elections, Republican candidates for governor, Chris Christie in New Jersey and Bob McDonnell in Virginia, won large victories seen as a rebuke to President

Obama. Conservatives and Republicans were fired up, and in a special election in Massachusetts in January 2010 to replace Senator Ted Kennedy, the unthinkable happened: a conservative Republican, Scott Brown, a former state legislator, won a surprise victory over his liberal female opponent in very liberal Massachusetts. Economic issues won the day for all of them, but Governor Christie and Senator Brown, who both support civil unions for gay and lesbian couples as well as other pro-equality measures, were also no doubt helped by their social tolerance in two heavily Democratic states.

While Democrats crowed about their victory with the health-care bill in March 2010, they were eating crow in November after their historic losses in the 2010 election. Republicans had won back sixty-three seats in the House and substantially increased their numbers in the US Senate, where they were now able to filibuster Democratic bills if necessary.

That election brought over eighty new House Republicans into office, most of them heavily identified with the Tea Party movement and more ideologically committed to the principles of limited government and free markets than any Congress in generations. Their challenge, and the Tea Party's challenge, during the 2012 election cycle will be to remain focused on the economic issues that brought them into office in 2010 by winning over the independents who decide elections, despite the constant focus of some of the Republican presidential candidates and their Religious Right supporters on issues like same-sex marriage and the Defense of Marriage Act. It will also be the challenge of libertarians and other supporters of social tolerance within the party to stay focused on the issues that put Republicans in charge of the House (and that might put them in charge of the Senate and the presidency in 2012), as well as to nudge the party toward a more tolerant position on gay issues. Again, most Republicans are already on board.[46]

With a few exceptions, the new House members have remained committed to focusing on economic issues during their first term. With all the contentious battles that lie ahead over taxes, spending, and reducing our huge deficit, they will need all the support from the public that they can muster, especially from political independents, who are firmly in the gay rights camp. Independents, like most of the country, are focused right now on economic issues, and rightfully so, but when the economy improves, as it surely will, other issues, like equal rights and social tolerance, will rise in importance to them and other voters. Republicans and conservatives who want to keep winning elections and build an enduring majority will forget that simple fact at their peril.

6

IS THE TEA PARTY NATION ANTI-GAY?

One of the most striking political developments since the election of President Barack Obama has been the birth of the Tea Party movement, perhaps the most momentous political development in the past several years. Exactly when this movement was born remains a point of contention, but many people trace it back to CNBC commentator Rick Santelli's electrifying February 19, 2009, on-air battle cry against a federal bailout for Americans who bought houses they couldn't afford and consequently could not pay their mortgages when the housing market crashed.[1]

Others, including supporters of libertarian presidential candidate Ron Paul, had spoken out in favor of tea parties and against the bailouts throughout 2008, as had other libertarians. Nevertheless, Santelli's justifiable rant against bailing out those homeowners, not to mention big banks and big business, struck a chord with the American people—not just Republicans but also independents across almost the entire political spectrum. The Tea Party movement as a national and broad-based phenomenon was born.

It is, for the most part, a decentralized coalition of organizations, activists, and aspiring politicians primarily from the right side of the political spectrum, ranging from libertarians to mainstream conservatives to right-wing populists to Christian conservatives. Millions of fed-up Americans have rallied under the Tea Party banner to take a stand against the enormous growth in federal spending and debt over the past decade, especially during the Obama administration.[2] And while a majority of Tea Party activists are Republican, many are independents, with even a few Democrats sprinkled among them.[3] In fact, according to a *Washington*

Post/ABC News poll released on November 9, 2011, the Tea Party is significantly less partisan than the Occupy Wall Street movement that blossomed in 2011 under the adoring gaze of the mainstream media. According to the poll, while six in ten Tea Party backers identified themselves as Republican, 70 percent of the Occupy Wall Street supporters labeled themselves as Democrats.[4]

Many of the Tea Party's grassroots organizers and activists came from outside the orbit of the conventional conservative movement, including many libertarians and conservatives who had grown disenchanted with the policies of President George W. Bush and the Republican Party. After all, it was Bush, with the assistance of most congressional Republicans, who increased domestic federal spending at a higher rate than even President Lyndon Johnson (one of the most profligate presidents in US history)[5] and instituted a major new entitlement, the Medicare prescription drug program. Most Tea Party activists see many of the Obama administration's programs and policies simply as extending those of the Bush administration, albeit at several times the cost.

Not surprisingly, the Tea Party movement has aroused the opposition and hatred of the liberal Left,[6] especially since fiery conservative politicians like Representative Michele Bachmann and Sarah Palin, as well as TV pundits Sean Hannity and Glenn Beck, have taken up its cause. Contrary to liberal conventional wisdom, however, the Tea Party movement is as much an insurgent movement within and against the Republican Party as it is against the progressive Left and President Obama. Its broad ideological makeup means it is a far more complex movement than its opponents, and even some of its supporters, realize. It has many strains and offshoots, but two main characteristics define it.

CORE BELIEFS OF THE TEA PARTY

The first main characteristic of the Tea Party is its overwhelming emphasis on economic, not social, issues.[7] From its very beginning, economic issues spurred its growth: government bailouts like the Troubled Asset Relief Program, the huge increases in federal debt, President Obama's health-care "reform" bill, the $1 trillion stimulus spending, and increased economic intervention have all added heat to the fire. Notably absent have been the social issues long associated with conservative religious organizations, such as abortion and gay rights, particularly gay marriage. As Kate Zernike wrote in the *New York Times* on March 12, 2010, "God, life, and family get little if any mention in [Tea Party] statements and manifestos. The motto of the Tea Party Patriots, a large coalition of tea party groups, is 'fiscal responsibility, limited government, and free market.'" She added, "Tea Party leaders argue that the nation can ill afford the discussion about social issues when it is passing on enormous debts to future generations. But the focus is also strategic: leaders think they can attract independent voters if they stay away from divisive issues."[8] That alone makes the Tea Party strikingly different from the bulk of the mainstream social conservative movement.

Leaving social issues off the table was and is sound strategy, and it is widely credited with the overwhelming Republican victory in the 2010 election.[9] With few exceptions, Tea Party activists, and Republicans in general, stayed on message during the midterm campaign. The Independence Caucus questionnaire, a generic questionnaire that many Tea Party groups used to evaluate political candidates prior to the 2010 election, contained eighty questions, mostly on the proper role of government and related policy questions. None of the questions were about social issues,[10] a telling contrast to Religious Right groups that focus almost exclusively on those issues.

Ryan Hecker, the organizer behind the Contract from America initiative, a manifesto of Tea Party beliefs and demands, believes that Tea Party organizers "should be creating the biggest tent possible around the economic conservative issues. I think social issues may matter to particular individuals, but at the end of the day, the movement should be agnostic about it. This is a movement that arose largely because the Republican Party failed to deliver on being representative of the economic conservative ideology. To include social issues would be beside the point."[11]

As a result, there has been little evidence of an overt anti-gay prejudice or agenda in the ranks or the leadership of the Tea Party movement, despite the various accusations from the Left that the movement is rife with homophobes and racists. In fact, many gay conservatives and gay Republicans have participated in the movement since its inception. Bruce Carroll, a blogger for the gay conservative GayPatriot website, says that in all the Tea Party events he's attended, he's never heard anti-gay statements. Mark Ciavola, the spokesman for another gay conservative blog called *Right Pride*, agrees. He also believes that engaging Tea Party activists about the economic issues and concerns they share is the best way to talk to them about other issues like gay rights.

This is not to say, of course, that most of the millions of Tea Party members are necessarily pro–gay rights, let alone pro–gay marriage. The various polls of the Tea Party's members that have been done on same-sex marriage, for example, show a level of support that varies but is about the same as, or a bit less than, that of Republicans at large, a quarter to a third of whom support same-sex marriage, according to recent polls.[12]

According to CBS News/*New York Times* polling released in April 2010, only 16 percent of Tea Party members polled supported gay marriage.[13] However, 41 percent supported civil unions, while 40 percent opposed both civil unions and gay marriage. That means that 57 percent supported some form of relationship recognition for gay couples, a far greater level of support than among the leaders of the Religious Right groups that make up much of the Republican base.

The Public Religion Research Institute's 2010 American Values Survey, the largest survey of its kind, reported similar findings: 18 percent for same-sex marriage (half the support in the general population, according to their poll, although that is a significantly lower level of support than in most of the polls conducted in 2011) and 45 percent opposed to any legal recognition of same-sex couples.[14] But 35 percent of Tea Party members supported civil unions,[15] which means a total of 53 percent supported relationship recognition of gay couples (either gay marriage or civil unions), an astonishing result in light of the common perception that Tea Party members are adamantly opposed to gay rights. In that same poll, 41 percent of Christian conservatives supported legal recognition of gay couples: 16 percent in favor of gay marriage and 27 percent for civil unions.[16] It appears that anti-gay organizations like the Family Research Council and the American Family Association don't even reflect the views of many members of the Christian Right.

Another, more recent poll by the Pew Forum on Religion & Public Life in early 2011 showed that support for same-sex marriage among Tea Party supporters had risen to 26 percent, with 64 percent opposed.[17] Given the earlier poll, which showed support for civil unions at at least 35 percent, combined support for either same-sex marriage or civil unions among Tea Party supporters had increased to perhaps 60 percent or more in the 2011 survey. While those numbers don't match the general public's support for same-sex marriage, they clearly indicate a significant difference between Tea Party supporters and the Religious Right on gay and lesbian issues.

That Pew Forum poll in fact concluded that "support for the Tea Party is not synonymous with support for the religious right."[18] In the 2010 PRRI poll, only 42 percent said they agreed with the conservative Christian movement, while 46 percent had not heard of it or had no opinion of it; 11 percent said they disagreed with it.[19] Clearly, the liberal argument that the Tea Party movement is a mirror image of the Religious Right is wildly incorrect, and gay rights advocates would be well advised to buck conventional wisdom and not write off the Tea Party movement as a source of measured support for their cause.

Despite their relatively low support for same-sex marriage, few Tea Party activists consider it a defining issue. A 2010 *Washington Post* survey of Tea Party groups across the country found that less than 1 percent of them consider same-sex marriage the single most important issue for their organization.[20] In fact, only two issues ranked lower in their list of priorities: abortion rights and gun rights. Fighting same-sex marriage is clearly not an important issue to most of them, a very different situation than in the leading social conservative organizations, for which it is often the top priority.

And in contrast to the angry response from most conservative organizations to the 2010 federal court ruling in Massachusetts overturning part of the Defense of Marriage Act (DOMA), the response of most Tea Party groups was quite muted. "The silence is by design," wrote Sandhya Somashekhar in the July 13, 2010, issue of the *Washington Post*, "because [the movement] is held together by an exclusive focus on fiscal matters and avoidance of divisive social issues such as abortion and gay marriage."[21] As discussed previously, in the Massachusetts case, Judge Joseph L. Tauro argued that Section 2 of DOMA violates the right of same-sex couples to equal protection under the law and therefore interferes with the traditional right of states to set their own marriage policies.

In fact, some Tea Party leaders publicly supported the decision by Judge Tauro because they agreed with the judge that it violated the

Constitution's Tenth Amendment, which grants states jurisdiction in matters like marriage. This decision, if it is upheld, has enormous implications for a whole host of federal interventions into state matters, and many conservatives understand and support the potential of this decision to overturn a long history of federal encroachment on states' rights. These are conservatives who are consistent in their support of federalism, even if they may disagree with how some states will handle the issue of gay marriage, a far cry from many in the Religious Right who put their anti-gay views above all else, states' rights be damned.

As Everett Wilkinson, state director for the Florida Tea Party Patriots, said, "On the issue of [gay marriage], we have no stance, but any time a state's rights or powers are encouraged over the federal government, it is a good thing."[22] Phillip Dennis, state coordinator for the Texas Tea Party Patriots, agreed: "I believe that if the people in Massachusetts want gay people to get married, then they should allow it, just as people in Utah do not support abortion. They should have the right to vote against that."[23] Judson Phillips, founder of the Tea Party Nation, acknowledged some of his members are also opposed to DOMA,[24] and Shelby Blakely of the Tea Party online publication called the *New Patriot Journal* said of Tauro's decision, "As far as an assertion of states' rights goes, I believe it's a good thing. . . . The Constitution does not allow federal regulation of gay marriage just as it doesn't allow for federal regulation of health care."[25] All these Tea Party activists provide more evidence of the gulf between the Tea Party and the Religious Right on this issue.[26]

Not surprising, many liberals also understand the implications of this decision. Yale University law professor Jack Balkin, for example, wrote that "as much as liberals might applaud the result, they should be aware that the logic of [Judge Tauro's] arguments, taken seriously, would undermine the constitutionality of wide swaths of federal regulatory programs and seriously constrict federal regulatory power."[27] Could there be any better reason to applaud Judge Tauro's decision?

Perhaps this understanding of the implications of the decision by the Tea Party helps explain why there was barely a peep from Tea Party activists over the Obama administration's March 2011 announcement that it would no longer defend DOMA in court, in striking contrast to the almost hysterical reaction from Religious Right groups like the Family Research Council, among others.

There is other evidence as well of a general tolerance on gay issues on the part of many Tea Party activists. A Montana Tea Party group recently kicked out one of its board members for remarks that seemingly condoned anti-gay violence. In Texas, a bastion of hard-core Republican conservative theocrats, the Republican Party recently replaced its "Schlaflyite culture warrior" chairman (in the words of author and journalist Jonathan Rauch) with a more traditional Reaganite who emphasized economic issues over social ones. As a Dallas Tea Party leader told Rauch, "We do not touch on social issues. We believe the biggest danger to the country is the fiscal irresponsibility that's going on in Washington."[28]

This more tolerant attitude on gay issues partly reflects the other main characteristic of the Tea Party movement: the strong and pervasive libertarian influence. Libertarians helped form the core of the early Tea Party movement, and they have struggled to keep it true to its roots, including a respect for equal rights under the law and social tolerance. The recent attention in the Tea Party movement paid to the Tenth and Fourteenth amendments, for example, is a by-product of the libertarian influence on both the movement and, increasingly, the Republican Party. Rarely were these amendments a topic of serious discussion in the past forty or fifty years in the Republican Party before they bubbled up from the grass roots in the past few years as an issue of great importance. These amendments are now the focus of intense discussion in the Republican Party and in the broader conservative movement thanks to the more libertarian elements of the Tea Party movement and its back-to-constitutional-basics philosophy.

Several studies have in fact documented the strong libertarian presence in the movement. One study, by David Kirby and Emily Ekins for the Cato Institute, found that roughly half of self-identified Tea Party members don't see a role for government in promoting "traditional values," a big reason the movement has been so focused on economic issues. These two researchers reported in a *Politico* article on October 28, 2010, that "just under half, or 48 percent, of tea partiers at the recent Virginia Tea Party Convention [the largest such convention to date] held views that are more accurately described as libertarian—fiscally conservative, to be sure, but moderate to liberal on social and cultural issues."[29] The other half, 51 percent, held the more traditional conservative view that government should promote "traditional values."[30] Kirby and Ekins also wrote that "tea party libertarians tend to be more independent and less loyal to the GOP than tea party conservatives, 69 percent for the latter versus just 39 percent for the libertarians."[31]

Their study reflects the findings of other analyses, such as a survey by *Politico*/TargetPoint that found a similar split between libertarians and conservatives.[32] And a 2010 *Washington Post*/Kaiser/Harvard survey found that respondents who supported or were leaning toward the Tea Party were split on social issues, with 42 percent characterized as moderate to liberal and 57 percent as conservative or very conservative.[33]

Even Glenn Beck, considered by many to be the father of the Tea Party movement, with a following numbering in the millions, expressed a surprisingly libertarian view of same-sex marriage on *The O'Reilly Factor* on August 13, 2010. Beck told viewers he does not believe it should be a political issue. "Honestly, I think we have bigger fish to fry,"[34] he said, and he mocked the idea that gay marriage poses a threat to the country by quoting Thomas Jefferson: "If it neither breaks my leg nor picks my pocket, what difference is it to me?" The fact that such an iconic figure in the Tea Party movement would express such views signals some fundamental change going on within the conservative movement regarding gay and lesbian rights.

WHICH WAY FOR THE TEA PARTY?

There is, in fact, a growing tension between libertarians and the more conservative and populist elements of the Tea Party movement, which in some states have gained ascendancy as the movement has grown. A number of the most successful, Tea Party–endorsed Republican candidates for the US Senate in 2010, for example, espoused some disturbing views on social issues like gay rights and the concept of the separation of church and state during their respective campaigns for the Senate. Republican candidates Sharron Angle in Nevada, Ken Buck in Colorado, and Christine O'Donnell in Delaware, for example, explicitly criticized the American tradition of the separation of church and state and urged more religious control over the government.[35] Angle was particularly outspoken in opposing gay rights, using slurs in public to refer to gay people and even stating that she would refuse money from corporate political action committees (PACs) affiliated with companies with pro-gay policies like domestic partner benefits, even though she took many contributions from noncorporate PACs that accepted donations from those same private companies. Given the fact that half of all Fortune 500 companies and 83 percent of Fortune 100 companies have such gay-friendly policies,[36] Angle's strident efforts to keep fighting the culture wars seem to have backfired, turning off more socially moderate business leaders and independents and helping lead to her defeat by Senator Harry Reid, once considered a political goner in Nevada, at least until Angle became the Republican nominee.

In the 2010 Republican primary race in Delaware, longtime Republican congressman Mike Castle, the preemptive favorite to beat Democrat Chris Coons in the general election, was narrowly defeated by Tea Party–backed neophyte Christine O'Donnell. Unfortunately, O'Donnell proved to be an intellectual lightweight whose outspoken personal views on homosexuality, masturbation, and witchcraft eclipsed her views on issues voters actually cared about. It is perhaps an unfortunate, if sometimes inevitable, by-product of the grassroots process that candidates like O'Donnell and Angle sometimes win primaries, only to be defeated by Democrats in general elections by losing the all-important independent vote. If the Tea Party movement wishes to stay true to its philosophical roots, it will need to remain vigilant against those who would steer it off course into pointless and ultimately self-defeating diversions into social issues. Even with the wind at their backs, these three candidates managed to lose their 2010 races, and their outspoken social views surely played a part in their defeats, especially in the case of O'Donnell.

This libertarian/conservative split in the Tea Party movement was further highlighted in a recent article titled "The Great Tea-Party Debate Is On,"[37] by Joseph Farah of the Far Right website WorldNetDaily (now called just WND). In it, Farah explicitly called for the Tea Party movement to subordinate economic issues to his version of the moral issues he believes we face, and he laid out a prescription for nothing less than a new American theocracy: "We are individuals accountable to a sovereign God who presides over the universe He created. . . . We need to be our brother's keeper. We need to recognize sin when we see it. We need to live by God's rules," he wrote.[38]

Keep in mind, this wasn't some local preacher speaking from his pulpit to parishioners who voluntarily entered his church; this was a political demand from someone who claims to believe in the traditional Republican values of individual liberty and free enterprise. Farah insists that the Tea Party movement should put the imposition of certain religious values at the top of its political agenda instead of the principles of economic freedom and limited government that have defined the Republican Party for generations. As the online libertarian publication *TIA Daily* put it, "He's proposing his own version of a hostile takeover: a hostile takeover of the Tea Party movement by the Christian Right."[39] Fortunately for the nation, the Tea Party movement and the Republican Party focused like a laser on economic issues during the 2010 elections, and the resulting victory stemmed from that focus.

Unfortunately, Farah is not alone in his attempt to drive a theocratic stake through the heart of the Tea Party movement. Former Alaska governor Sarah Palin had taken up the same battle cry even before Farah spoke out, telling a group of evangelicals in April 2010, "Lest anyone try to convince you that God should be separated from the state, our founding fathers, they were believers."[40] But as Cato Institute vice president Gene Healy responded, "They were, but so what? Those believers deliberately crafted 'a Godless Constitution,'"[41] something the conservative theocrats either just can't seem to comprehend or refuse to acknowledge.

Likewise, Representative John Fleming (R-LA) felt compelled to warn the American people that either we "remain a Christian nation" or we head "down the socialist road" to "a godless society."[42] This fire-and-brimstone rhetoric may play well in some churches, but it is completely inappropriate for a political rally and will drive millions of independents and libertarians away from both the Republican Party and the Tea Party movement if it begins to dominate their shared agenda. That has happened before, and it will again, if we allow the Religious Right once more to become the face of the Republican Party by diverting our attention from economic issues, the issues that the Republican Party today is thriving on.

These naked attempts by extreme social conservatives to repudiate the libertarian essence of the Tea Party movement are a travesty, and there can be no clearer line in the sand between those who genuinely believe in the principles of freedom that this country was founded upon and interlopers like Farah and others who have an entirely different vision for this country. Libertarians and true conservatives must fight that vision tooth and nail.

There is some evidence that Tea Party and Republican activists have learned the lesson of the overwhelming Republican victory in the 2010 election and are acting accordingly. On November 16, 2010, a gay conservative organization called GOProud joined hands with various Tea Party activists to circulate a letter to Republican congressional leaders urging them to keep their focus in the new Congress on shrinking the federal government and to ignore those in the party who want to focus more on social issues.[43] As Chris Barron, founder of the group, wrote in the letter, "This election was not a mandate for the Republican Party, nor was it a mandate to act on any social issue." Ralph King, a Tea Party Patriots national leadership council member and a signer of the letter, told the Washington newspaper *Politico*, "When they were out in the Boston Harbor, they weren't arguing about who was gay or who was having an abortion. I look at myself as pretty socially conservative. But that's not what we push through the Tea Party Patriots."[44] A rival group of Tea Party groups and organizations also sent a letter to Speaker John Boehner with a list of its "demands," likewise focusing exclusively on fiscal and economic policy except for one issue: it called for reinstatement of Don't Ask, Don't Tell, the now-repealed policy of not allowing openly gay service members in our armed forces.[45] The letter stated, "This policy has worked well for the last fifteen years. There is no reason to change." Given that a majority of Republicans and an overwhelming majority of the American people supported the repeal, the House leadership has no intention of actually attempting such a reversal, but it's unfortunate that this silly "demand" was included at all.

Other Republican leaders, such as Governor Haley Barbour of Mississippi and Governor Mitch Daniels of Indiana, both at one time considered possible presidential candidates, have called for a moratorium on talking about social issues, and they have been attacked for their views. It will be instructive to see how other Republican leaders and Tea Party activists react in the long term to this initiative by GOProud and its allies in the Tea Party movement and the Republican Party.

In an age when Americans are becoming more socially tolerant and less religious, blatantly homophobic views are increasingly out of step with most voters, and rightfully so. Tea Party–backed Republicans with such extreme views who run for office will lose votes from the very people whom Republicans in most cases won back in the last election—independents, suburban voters, and women—just as they did in the 2008 election.

The tension between the libertarian and conservative/populist elements of the Tea Party movement, as well as within the Republican Party, will persist, but evidence is mounting that more and more Republicans, including a few of the Republican presidential candidates, are tiring of the overt religiosity of some on the right and beginning to speak out. The dustup in July 2011 over the so-called Marriage Vow, distributed to the Republican field of presidential candidates in Iowa by an extremist group called The Family Leader, illustrates this hopeful trend.

Iowa is famous, of course, for its first-in-the-nation presidential caucus, and the politics of most Iowa Republican caucus voters skew sharply to the right—in some cases, to the extreme right. They like their hard-core social views almost as much as they like their ethanol subsidies: they can't get enough of either one. But with the Marriage Vow,[46] some of them may have overreached, even in Iowa. After succinctly outlining (correctly) some of the consequences of the breakdown of the two-parent family structure caused by welfare-state dependency over the past several decades, the Marriage Vow veers off into a broad attack on homosexuality in particular, as well as on modern sexual mores and beliefs in general. It demands of the signer fidelity not just to his or her own spouse but also to a wide variety of authoritarian and statist measures meant to engineer our society back into the safe and predictable Christian-dominated society so many of the vow's proponents cherished and grew up in. It calls for everything from downsizing America's huge public debt and unfunded liabilities to a full-throated attack on homosexuality, same-sex marriage or civil unions, pornography, divorce, prostitution, infidelity, and even Muslim sharia law.[47] Many older Americans no doubt pine for the "good old days" of the 1950s, but their battle to take America back to that time is a losing one.

If the Marriage Vow's creators expected all the presidential candidates to fall meekly into line, they were sadly mistaken. It was not surprising, of course, that Rick Santorum and Michele Bachmann signed it before the ink was dry: both have a long history of anti-gay statements and public expressions of their personal faith. It was surprising, however, that all of the other candidates then in the race refused to sign it, for a variety of reasons. It was an unexpected and widespread rebuke of the vow and the group behind it.

The candidates had a variety of reasons for withholding their signatures: Jon Huntsman doesn't sign pledges—any pledges. Mitt Romney found the rhetoric in some of the demands offensive. Tim Pawlenty wanted to put his vow into his own words and so issued his own appropriately composed paean to his religious faith. Ron Paul diplomatically said he disagreed with some of its proposals; as he is a libertarian, that was not surprising. Others simply refused to sign. Surely the most remarkable response, however, came from former New Mexico governor Gary Johnson, who issued a frontal assault on the vow from an explicitly libertarian perspective.

Calling it "offensive and un-Republican,"[48] Johnson denounced the pledge as a call to discriminate against anyone who makes a personal choice that doesn't meet the group's definition of virtue. "The Republican Party cannot afford to have a Presidential candidate who condones intolerance, bigotry, and the denial of liberty to the citizens of this country,"[49] he added. Not since Religious Right activists became the base of the Republican Party has any presidential candidate issued such a stinging rebuke to the theocrats who have had such a grip on the Republican Party for the last few decades. "In one concise document," Johnson concluded, "they manage to condemn gays, single parents, single individuals, divorcees, Muslims, gays in the military, unmarried couples, women who choose to have an abortion, and everyone else who doesn't fit in a Norman Rockwell painting."[50]

The philosophical tensions and differences that permeate the broader conservative movement may ultimately strengthen it by clarifying the fundamental constitutional issues involved, but they could also tear the movement apart if social conservatives continue to put the primacy of their anti-gay agenda above the core values of limited government and free enterprise that everyone agrees upon. Libertarians and others who want to keep the movement's focus strictly on economic issues must aggressively challenge those who would take the movement and the Republican Party in the wrong direction by ignoring this country's fundamentally libertarian heritage, and that won't be easy.

In 2011, half of the Tea Party Caucus members in the House of Representatives, for example, signed on as co-sponsors of H. Con. Res. 25, a bill that condemns the Obama administration's 2011 decision to stop defending the Defense of Marriage Act in court and demands "that the Department of Justice continue to defend the Defense of Marriage Act in all instances."[51] As of mid-2011, twenty-six members of the fifty-two-member Tea Party Caucus had signed up as co-sponsors of the bill, despite the fact that DOMA directly contravenes the Tenth Amendment by undercutting the right of each state to determine its own marriage laws. As Margaret Talbot wrote in the February 24, 2011, issue of the *New Yorker*, DOMA was "a radical departure"[52] from the traditional policy of state control over this issue. As public opinion moves further and further away from the views of social conservatives on gay rights, they will ramp up their rhetoric and their pressure on Tea Party members and conservative activists, particularly those in Congress, to defend their anti-gay agenda.

The more that Republicans, conservatives, and libertarians focus on the economic issues that unite us, the sooner we will reach our goals of smaller government, lower taxes, and more personal freedom. Ultimately, however, supporters of legal equality for gays and lesbians must impress upon all Republicans that support for gay rights is an integral part of the pro-freedom, limited government philosophy we all profess to believe in.

7

WHERE DO WE GO FROM HERE?

On September 22, 2010, an important political fund-raiser was held at a chic Manhattan residence. It featured many prominent Republican conservatives: former Republican National Committee (RNC) chairman Ken Mehlman and former solicitor general (under President George W. Bush) Ted Olson were two of the best-known attendees. Other prominent Republicans there included Mary Cheney, the openly gay daughter of former vice president Dick Cheney; Steve Schmidt, a senior campaign advisor to Senator John McCain's presidential campaign; AT&T's Jim Cicconi, a former staffer for Karl Rove; GOP donor and hedge fund manager Paul E. Singer; Peter Thiel, a California venture capitalist and Ron Paul supporter; former New Jersey governor Christine Todd Whitman; former Massachusetts governor William Weld; former RNC counsel Benjamin Ginsberg; former Federal Election Commission chairman Michael Toner; former Bush communications adviser and TV pundit Nicolle Wallace; Israel Hernandez, longtime aide to the Bush family; and Margaret Hoover, a former Bush campaign advisor and Fox News contributor.

There was nothing all that remarkable about this event except for one thing: it was a fund-raiser for the American Foundation for Equal Rights, a bipartisan national organization promoting same-sex marriage.[1] Although an event like this, with so many Republicans and conservatives in attendance, would have been inconceivable just a few years ago, here they were on behalf of marriage equality for gay and lesbian Americans. Mehlman, who was also George W. Bush's 2004 campaign manager, had just publicly come out shortly before the event,[2] and Ted Olson was fresh off his historic win in the California Supreme Court case that ended with the ruling declaring that Proposition 8, passed by California voters in 2008 to outlaw same-sex marriage, was unconstitutional.

This fund-raiser was but one sign of the dramatic changes taking place not just in American society but also in the Republican Party on the issue of expanding gay and lesbian rights and even on the issue of marriage rights. And other recent Republican events illustrate just as clearly the remarkable changes going on in the Republican Party and the conservative movement on this issue.

That same evening, in fact, another Republican fund-raiser was taking place in Washington, DC, at the Republican Party's Capitol Hill Club, located next to the RNC headquarters and just blocks from the Capitol building. Log Cabin Republicans, a national gay and lesbian Republican organization of about nineteen thousand members, were having their annual dinner, and helping host the VIP reception at the dinner on behalf of Log Cabin's congressional political action committee (as well as receiving an award) was none other than Senator John Cornyn from Texas, chairman of the National Republican Senatorial Committee.[3] Even though he was urged by social conservatives like Tony Perkins from the Family Research Council to boycott the event, Cornyn refused to bend, saying he wanted to affirm "the basic dignity of every human life, including not only unborn children, but also adults with whom we may disagree. I believe we are all made in the image and likeness of God."[4] Also receiving an award at that same event was Representative Pete Sessions, chairman of the National Republican Congressional Committee. Although he was not in attendance, he sent a video greeting to the dinner participants thanking them for their support of Republican efforts in the election.[5]

The participation of these two gentlemen who are at the pinnacle of Republican House and Senate leadership was unprecedented and offered fresh evidence that Republican leaders are finally beginning to understand that American culture is changing rapidly and that the Republican Party must change with it in order to survive and grow. Following the historic Republican win on Election Day 2010, it was probably also not lost on them that exit polls that day showed that fully a third of gay and lesbian voters supported Republican candidates.[6]

The changes in the Republican Party were also evident earlier in 2010 at one of the conservative movement's premiere events: the annual

Conservative Political Action Conference (CPAC) held in Washington, DC, sponsored by the American Conservative Union (ACU) and virtually every other major conservative organization. Thousands of conservative activists—ranging from Ronald Reagan Republicans to unreconstructed Goldwaterites and libertarians to social conservatives and the fringes beyond—meet to hear speeches, attend seminars and workshops, and listen to potential Republican presidential candidates and current Republican officeholders. There usually is little that deviates from the standard conservative positions or talking points about almost every major political topic, from taxes to national defense to judicial activism and the sanctity of life.

But the 2010 CPAC conference was a refreshing and remarkable change. For the first time ever, a pro-gay conservative organization called GOProud was one of many co-sponsors of the conference. When several of the usual sponsoring organizations objected to having a pro-gay organization in attendance and threatened to pull out unless GOProud was kicked out, the organizers refused to back down. GOProud stayed as a sponsoring organization and was welcomed by all but a few of the other organizations and attendees at the conference.[7]

But that wasn't the end of it. The 2010 event boasted a larger than usual libertarian contingent, including many members of a student libertarian organization called Students for Liberty, headed by a young activist named Alexander McCobin, also a speaker. At the end of his remarks about student organizing to an audience of a thousand or so attendees, McCobin spoke out in support of GOProud's presence at the conference and thanked the organizers for welcoming them. Although he received some heckling from the audience, he explicitly praised those who are socially tolerant as well as fiscally responsible. "Students today recognize that freedom does not come in pieces. It is a single concept that we must defend at all times,"[8] McCobin said. His courage paid off, because he received a surprisingly positive response from the audience full of young conservative and libertarian activists.

Minutes later, however, another student speaker, Ryan Sorba from Young Americans for Freedom, responded angrily to McCobin's remarks and condemned CPAC for allowing GOProud to attend the conference. Much of the audience erupted into boos and catcalls as Sorba's remarks disintegrated into a hateful screed against gay rights and homosexuality.[9]

The presence of GOProud at CPAC and the exchange between McCobin and Sorba all but dominated convention discussions during the entire event, and their clash symbolized better than anything else the growing visibility and acceptance of gay rights by Republican Party and conservative movement activists, albeit the more libertarian ones. The presence of Sorba and numerous other anti-gay organizations and activists at CPAC, however, also highlighted the challenges we still face in the Republican Party and conservative movement regarding tolerance of gays and lesbians.

In fact, the 2010 confrontation presaged an even bigger split at the 2011 CPAC conference, when a number of anti-gay social conservative organizations explicitly boycotted the event because of the presence of GOProud.[10] The Family Research Council, the National Organization for Marriage, the American Principles Project, the Capital Research Center, the Heritage Foundation, and the Center for Military Readiness, an organization whose sole focus has been to fight the repeal of Don't Ask, Don't Tell, issued a joint statement condemning the participation of GOProud, criticizing David Keene, then executive director of the ACU, and other board members for promoting "moral surrender" on the issue of marriage.

The split did not appear to keep many activists from the 2011 conference, however, which saw its biggest crowd yet (and an even larger libertarian contingent), with over eleven thousand in attendance. Even some social conservatives chided the boycotting organizations for their petulant actions. Pete Wehner, senior fellow at the Ethics and Public Policy Center and a member of the Reagan administration and both Bush administrations, wrote that the boycotters came "across as defensive and insecure, as if they fear that their arguments cannot win the day on the merits,"[11] and he characterized their efforts as "small-minded and unwise."[12] Although a number of CPAC speakers tried to promote the traditional fusion of economic, social, and national security conservatives, the die may be cast for a growing split between the extreme social conservatives in the party, who put their personal moral values above all else, and those who want to grow the Republican Party by forging an alliance with libertarian and socially tolerant voters who share the longtime Republican principles of individual liberty and limited government.

Unfortunately, a number of prominent individuals and organizations in the social conservative movement have explicitly attacked a pro-freedom agenda that combines fiscal conservatism and responsibility with social tolerance, making it clear that their top allegiance is to their personal religious values rather than to the free market principles, limited government, and individual rights that all those on the right supposedly share.

Matt Barber from Liberty Counsel, for example, attacked GOProud for "pushing a radical leftist agenda that is an affront to the GOP platform, conservatism, and, most importantly, the Word of God." According to Barber, this "radical" agenda includes support of "both 'gay marriage' and 'civil unions,' [opposition to] pro-marriage constitutional amendments, pushing for repeal of Don't Ask, Don't Tell, and advocating for federal 'partnership benefits' for federal employees."[13]

Yet, as discussed in previous chapters, with the possible exception of same-sex marriage, all of these positions are supported by most libertarians, and most of them also command support from a majority of mainstream Republican voters. Polling has shown repeatedly that at least half of Republican voters support either civil unions or same-sex marriage and that this number is growing. Polls have also consistently shown that a majority of both Republicans and conservatives opposed Don't Ask, Don't Tell, a policy that was finally repealed in 2010.

Opposition to the Federal Marriage Amendment (FMA) has been, and continues to be, widespread among conservatives on federalism grounds, and today such an amendment is rarely promoted even among the Far Right groups that used to make it a top priority. While polls in 2004 and 2006 showed more Republicans than not supporting the FMA, many prominent Republicans, such as Vice President Dick Cheney, Senator John McCain (AZ), Governor George Pataki (NY), Representative Ron Paul (TX), former New York City mayor Rudy Giuliani, and Representative Bob Barr (GA), among others, all opposed the amendment on the grounds that marriage law has been and should remain a state issue. Notably, Representative Barr was the author of the Defense of Marriage Act back in 1996, but he now strongly opposes it. Should all of these gentlemen have been kicked out of CPAC and the conservative movement for their "radical leftist agenda," as Barber demanded for GOProud? Clearly, Barber and his colleagues on the extreme right fail to understand that they command the support of just a small slice of the American electorate, a slice that is shrinking every year.

The myopia exhibited by Liberty Counsel and other like-minded organizations is almost laughable, except that it could have dire consequences for the future of the Republican Party. Indeed, if anyone is promoting a "radical agenda" that is out of step with mainstream America and even most Republicans, it is Far Right organizations like Liberty Counsel, the Family Research Council, and the other boycotting organizations that make opposition to gay rights the cornerstone of their legislative agendas.

It remains to be seen what will happen in the future with CPAC and in the broader conservative movement. After the 2011 CPAC convention, Keene was replaced by the former chairman of the Florida Republican Party, Al Cardenas, who publicly lamented the absence of the Heritage Foundation and the other boycotting organizations at the 2011 convention. He and his new board decided in 2011 that GOProud would not be welcomed back as a co-sponsor,[14] but that action will certainly cause its own backlash, and rightfully so. Perhaps some accommodation will be made that allows all groups, including GOProud, to attend and exhibit at CPAC, but as of this writing, it remains to be seen how this issue will impact the 2012 event. Caving in to bullies, however, is never a good strategy, and placating them by restricting who can attend or co-sponsor CPAC will simply embolden them and reinforce the widely held stereotype of the typical conservative voter and activist as intolerant and afraid to confront other viewpoints.

The larger and more important struggle over control of the Republican Party and the conservative movement will go on. Mainstream Republicans, conservatives, and libertarians now face a unique political challenge and an opportunity for growth, one that rarely presents itself in such a big way. The overtly leftist ideology of President Barack Obama and the previous Democrat-controlled Congress sparked a rather severe political realignment in 2010, one that we can all build on with the right strategic vision and policies. As we have seen, a variety of voter groups—women, suburbanites, independents, and even many younger voters—who had progressively deserted Republicans over the past fifteen or twenty years, partly in reaction to the right-wing culture wars, came back in a big way to the Republican Party in both 2009 and 2010,[15] presumably including the 20 percent of self-identified conservatives who supported Senator Obama in his 2008 presidential campaign. With the right message, Republicans can hold on to those voters in 2012 and beyond.

Whereas independents had favored Democrats by eighteen percentage points in the 2006 election, for example, by 2010, Republicans had bested Democrats with a 56 to 37 percent edge among independents.[16] These voters came back because of a campaign by Republicans and Tea Party groups that relentlessly focused on the economic concerns that most people care about, not on divisive social issues. Independents, women, and younger voters are all pro–gay rights and pro-tolerance, so any attempt to revive or expand the culture war could have devastating consequences for the party by chipping away at these voters' support for Republican candidates and policies. The Republican Party will lose them again if we allow our party's leaders and elected representatives to go back to being Pied Pipers for the Religious Right.

A June 25, 2010, Gallup poll measuring ideological affiliation, after all, found that while 42 percent of adults consider themselves conservative, 35 percent consider themselves moderate (with just 20 percent as liberal), including a quarter of Republicans.[17] But among independents, the largest group of voters, the breakdown is almost reversed, with 41 percent calling themselves moderate and 36 percent conservative.[18] Clearly, a candidate who identifies with the hard Right and its priorities of opposing gay rights, further regulating abortion, and increasing religious influence on public policy will have a hard time attracting the independent support he or she will need.

Even many (perhaps most) self-identified libertarian voters—perhaps 10 to 15 percent or more of the electorate[19]—will likely desert the party in the event that it nominates an anti-gay candidate. According to the Pew Research Center, "fully 67 percent of libertarians self-identify as independents, compared to 28 percent as Republicans and 5 percent as Democrats."[20] The Republican Party cannot take their votes for granted simply because President Obama is the Democratic candidate.

In fact, writers from across the political spectrum agree that independents are the key to a Republican victory in 2012. Writing in the October

29, 2011, issue of *National Journal*, for example, political analyst Ronald Brownstein said, "The number of Americans who identify as independents now sometimes exceeds the number who align with Republicans or Democrats. . . . The population of truly untethered independents remains large enough to usually decide national elections, as they did for Democrats in 2006 and 2008 and then for Republicans in 2010."[21]

Given the ongoing demographic changes among US voters, those independents will only grow in importance to the Republican Party. In a 2011 study for the liberal think tank Center for American Progress, political analysts Ruy Teixeira and John Halpin discussed their data showing that the 2008 electorate that gave President Obama his substantial victory was only 74 percent white, with the other 26 percent composed primarily of Hispanic and black voters.[22]

In 2012, that slice of minority voters will be at least two percentage points higher, increasing even more the importance of white independents to the Republicans. Furthermore, the "two groups that will be critical to Obama's reelection are younger voters and single women," Teixeira and Halpin added.[23] It will be critically important for Republicans to peel off as many of those voters as possible, but virtually all of the polling data show that Republicans will not be able to do that if the party's message is one of outspoken intolerance for gay and lesbian Americans. Indeed, such a message could easily tip the election toward President Obama unless the economy seriously deteriorates in 2012.

Unfortunately, there are a number of potential Republican candidates for president who seem determined to prostrate themselves before the most extreme religious conservatives, those who unfortunately still play a disproportionate role in the Republican presidential nomination process. We saw that groveling in Iowa and other early primary states by candidates who try to outdo each other in their stated fealty to God, religion, and a revival of the culture wars.

This, then, will be the challenge for all Republicans, including libertarians and traditional conservatives, not just in 2012 but also over the next few years: to break the grip on the Republican Party of those with a narrow religious agenda as opposed to those who believe in the ideals of liberty, limited government, and personal freedom for all. That means we must welcome everyone who believes in those core principles into our party and then apply those principles across the board to everyone, including gay and lesbian Americans. Together, united around those beliefs and focused on the economic issues that most people care about, Republicans can defeat and repeal the harmful policies of President Obama and the Democrats and return this nation to the principles that made it great, including the principle of equal protection under the law.

8

A LAST HURRAH FOR REPUBLICAN ANTI-GAY BIGOTRY?

Despite the nation's and the Republican Party's changing views on gay rights, including support for relationship recognition for gay couples, the 2012 Republican presidential field is the most Far Right on social issues in modern US history, and a detailed review of the positions of the top social conservative candidates reveals a very dark side not only of their views about gay rights but also of their longtime associations with professional hate organizations, even individuals whose incendiary rhetoric could incite violence against gay and lesbian Americans.

Ironically, however, because a large field of Republican contenders is seeking the nomination, there are also more pro–gay rights candidates this time around than ever before. This irony is the result of a unique confluence of political and philosophical changes taking place: rapidly changing social views about gays and lesbians running head long into the growing dissatisfaction about the economy among most voters and the unprecedented recent growth in conservative and libertarian attitudes about the proper role of government in our lives and in the economy, including the birth of the Tea Party.

An analysis of the positions on gay and lesbian issues held by the Republican contenders for president, both those still in the race and those who have dropped out, reveals a great deal about the various factions and organizations that are part of the party's base and driving the party's agenda on social issues. Most of these contenders are totally out of sync with most Americans (and, in most cases, Republicans as well) on almost every gay rights issue. This analysis will also tell us where the party might be headed in terms of not just gay and lesbian rights but also the broader issue of social tolerance.

RICK PERRY

Although Governor Rick Perry is now the second-longest-serving governor in the country, few had heard much about him since he took the reins of power in Texas after George W. Bush won the White House in 2000—that is, until recently. He came to the attention of so many Americans before he actually entered the race for the Republican nomination because of a religious rally called "The Response" that he organized and headlined for on August 6, 2011, at Reliant Stadium in Houston, Texas. The rally reveals a great deal about his core beliefs and deep-seated bigotry.

Billed as a nondenominational, nonpolitical Christian prayer rally and officially called a "Call to Prayer for a Nation in Crisis," it was in fact a who's who of Religious Right organizations and spokesmen, many of them euphemistically labeled "wingnuts" in modern political jargon—that is, Far Right religious extremists who see politics not as a process of simply choosing our leaders and public policies based on specific political beliefs but as a means to conduct a religious crusade with the ultimate goal of instituting a Christian theocracy.

That description certainly applies to the American Family Association (AFA),[1] the organization that paid for the rally. Headed by Reverend Tim Wildmon, the AFA is based in Mississippi and known for its extreme hatred of homosexuals and efforts to deny them whatever rights it can. The AFA's chief spokesman is Bryan Fischer, its director of issues analysis for government and public policy and host of its radio show. Fischer has a long history of making radical statements about gays and lesbians, as well as other people outside the AFA's circle of true believers.[2]

Fischer has stated that gay people were responsible for the Holocaust,[3] that Adolf Hitler was gay,[4] and that gay activists are "domestic terrorists."[5] He has also called gay people Nazis intent on committing "virtual genocide" against the military because they supported the repeal of Don't Ask, Don't Tell (DADT),[6] and he has stated on his radio show that they should be disqualified from holding public office.[7] But gays and lesbians aren't the only Americans Fischer and the AFA hate.

Fischer has also said that Muslims should "have no First Amendment claims" to freedom of religion and should be deported;[8] that Native

Americans are "morally disqualified" from living in this country because they never converted to Christianity and were therefore cursed by God to a life of poverty and alcoholism;[9] that African American women "rut like rabbits" due to welfare benefits;[10] and that the anti-Muslim views of Anders Breivik, the Norwegian terrorist who killed nearly one hundred men, women, and children in 2011, were "accurate."[11] Perhaps it's because of these statements and many others by AFA officials that the Southern Poverty Law Center has labeled it a hate group. Yet these are the kind of people Governor Perry (as well as some of the other Republican contenders) has freely chosen to associate with, including sharing their views, on a continuing basis going back many years.

Perry's first association with the AFA, in fact, occurred in 2005 when he invited AFA founder Donald Wildmon to a signing ceremony celebrating the state's passage of a constitutional amendment defining marriage as between one man and one woman. Even though Perry's signature as governor was not even required by Texas law, he wanted to publicize his support for the amendment.[12] He also invited a radical, anti-gay minister, Rod Paisley, to speak at the ceremony.[13] Paisley spewed long-discredited "facts" about homosexuality derived from the "research" conducted by one Dr. Paul Cameron, a Far Right quack who was kicked out of both the American Psychological Association and the American Sociological Association, which stated that Cameron "consistently misinterpreted and misrepresented sociological research on sexuality, homosexuality, and lesbianism."[14] After Paisley finished his remarks, the delighted governor thanked him for "protecting the children of Texas from the gay agenda,"[15] thus repeating and promoting the Far Right lie that gays and lesbians target children.

Also present at both that religious rally in Houston as well as the 2005 signing ceremony was another of the leading anti-gay organizations in the country, the Family Research Council (FRC), a spin-off of James Dobson's Focus on the Family group, which lobbies in Washington and around the country on a variety of social conservative issues, focusing primarily on its anti-gay and anti-abortion agenda. FRC has been headed since 2003 by a former Louisiana state legislator named Tony Perkins, who is a frequent guest on TV and radio promoting anti-gay legislation and views. He has called gay activists everything from hateful and vile to "pawns of Satan."[16] When Congress repealed the DADT policy in the spring of 2011, he led a campaign to reverse the repeal and wrote that Congress would have "the blood of innocent soldiers on their hands"[17] if it allowed gay soldiers to serve. When gay teen suicide became a national issue in 2011 after several highly publicized gay suicides, Perkins said that gay teens who commit suicide do so because they know they are "abnormal," not because they are bullied.[18]

Like his colleagues in the Religious Right movement, Perkins adamantly rejects the concept of the separation of church and state, calling those who support this quintessentially American value "cultural terrorists."[19] When asked by the *Washington Examiner* about the distinction between preaching from the pulpit versus using the political process to advance his religious views, he said both are equally important.[20] And in that same interview, he stated that in his view (and those of his followers), religious liberty means imposing his interpretation of the scriptures on society,[21] a radically different, almost Orwellian view of what religious liberty actually means to most Americans.

Considering his long association with organizations on the extreme Right, then, it is no surprise that Perry has a long record of opposing equal rights for gays and lesbians. Besides supporting the prohibition of any legal recognition of gay couples, he even supports reinstating state sodomy laws, even though the US Supreme Court declared them unconstitutional in 2003.[22]

Advocates of equality saw a glimmer of hope for Perry when he stated at a Republican gathering in 2011 that if states like New York want to have gay marriage (the state had just legalized it), that was okay with him: "Our friends in New York six weeks ago passed a statute that said marriage can be between two people of the same sex. And you know what? That's New York, and that's their business, and that's fine with me."[23] That belief would be consistent with the traditional Republican view of states' rights and federalism. But Perry was quickly taken to the woodshed by Tony Perkins and shortly thereafter renounced that position, stating that he supports passage of the Federal Marriage Amendment,[24] which would outlaw same-sex marriage nationwide regardless of what each state decided on the matter, proving that he is a political opportunist above all else. He supports the Defense of Marriage Act (DOMA) and opposes any effort to equalize work-related benefits for gay and lesbian federal employees. He would also work to overturn the repeal of DADT.[25]

There is simply no doubt that a Perry presidency would be a disaster for gay and lesbian rights.

Rating: F

MITT ROMNEY

One of the primary criticisms of former Massachusetts governor Mitt Romney since he began running for president in 2007 has been that he's a serial flip-flopper on a variety of issues, particularly social issues like gay rights and abortion. And Romney's actions and words during the 2012 presidential primary season have done nothing but reinforce that perception.

Governor Romney was once somewhat supportive of gay rights, though not nearly to the extent that his opponents like to say. When running for the Senate against Ted Kennedy in 1994, he told gay voters he would be a stronger proponent of gay rights than Kennedy himself and that he supported protections against employment discrimination, telling them, "We must make equality for gays and lesbians a mainstream concern."[26] This is an admirable and certainly long-overdue sentiment, to be sure. During that same campaign, he favored allowing gays to serve openly in the military,[27] but he has since repudiated that position.

During his term as governor, however, Romney did little to promote equality for gays and lesbians at the state level, and he consistently opposed same-sex marriage when his state's supreme court declared its law against it unconstitutional in 2003. He tried on several occasions to overturn the court's decision, and he has consistently supported a federal marriage amendment as far back as 2004.[28]

He has been somewhat more supportive on other gay issues, for example, in 2002 stating support for domestic partnership rights such as health benefits and inheritance rights.[29] In 2007, he stated support for state-level employment nondiscrimination statutes,[30] and during an October 2011 campaign stop in New Hampshire, he stated his support for "partnership agreements" incorporating limited legal rights for gay couples.[31]

And in stark contrast to his many anti-gay statements to voters in Iowa and other socially conservative states, Romney told the *Nashua Telegraph* on November 21, 2011, while campaigning in New Hampshire, "I'm in favor of traditional marriage, I oppose same-sex marriage. At the same time, I don't believe in discriminating in employment or opportunity for gay individuals. So I favor gay rights, I do not favor same-sex marriage. That has been my position all along."[32]

These were certainly welcome words from someone who has too often read from the same anti-gay script as most of the other Republican candidates since he began running for president four years ago. Unfortunately, his beliefs about gay rights seem to change depending on which audience he's talking to. Along with Michele Bachmann, Rick Santorum, and Tim Pawlenty, for example, he signed a pledge from the National Organization for Marriage (NOM) in August 2011 promising to support a federal marriage amendment to the US Constitution, defend DOMA in court, nominate Supreme Court judges who oppose gay marriage, and even establish a presidential commission on "religious liberty" that would investigate alleged threats and intimidation against opponents of same-sex marriage.[33] Other presidential candidates, such as Ron Paul, Jon Huntsman, and Gary Johnson, refused to sign it for varying reasons.

NOM, by the way, is another extreme right-wing organization that opposes not just same-sex marriage but all equal rights for gays and lesbians, including employment nondiscrimination and allowing gays to serve openly in the military. All you need to know about this organization is that after the East Coast earthquake on August 24, 2011, one of its board members, Rabbi Yehuda Levin, claimed that "one of the reasons God brings earthquakes to the world is because of the transgressions of homosexuality."[34] But he didn't stop there: "Yes, there is a direct connection between earthquakes and homosexuality. There was in Haiti and it is here, in New York, in Washington, DC, where they passed homosexual legislation ordinances, in New York City and state, where they opened, especially on Sunday early, where they passed the homosexual marriage law."[35] These are the folks whom some of our presidential candidates are so eager to please.

Given his record of flip-flopping on gay rights issues (and others), it's hard to say what Governor Romney really believes. Who can trust what he says given his desire to do and say whatever it takes to get the Republican nomination?

Rating: D+

MICHELE BACHMANN

It is a testament to the Tea Party's power and influence on the Republican Party that Representative Michele Bachmann became a serious contender for the Republican nomination for president, if only for a short time. Ever since she entered Congress in 2006 as a representative from Minnesota, she has been a relentless advocate for smaller government and cutting federal spending and taxes, something all of us support. But she has, like some of the other Republican contenders, a very dark side when it comes to individual freedom and legal equality for gay and lesbian Americans, based at least in part on her extreme religious views, which she often mentions on the campaign trail.[36] Christian Dominionism, as it is often called, is an obscure religious sect of sorts based on the theological writings of Francis Schaeffer, a theologian and author of *The Christian Manifesto* who died in 1984. Schaeffer promoted a kind of theocracy in which Christians are commanded to run the government based on the Bible, which represents the total truth. For that reason, he argued, Christians alone are biblically mandated to run otherwise secular governmental institutions.[37] Although still not widely known, even among evangelicals, Schaeffer influenced thousands of hard-core fundamentalists, and his call to overthrow the US government if *Roe v. Wade*[38] is not overturned has presumably influenced some of the more radical factions in the anti-abortion movement.

Early in her political career, Bachmann promoted a virulently anti-gay message, despite the fact that her half sister is a lesbian. During the 2004 election in Minnesota, in order to pass that state's constitutional amendment against gay marriage, she routinely denounced the gay "lifestyle"[39] and claimed that, referring to the gay and lesbian community in Minnesota, "it is our children who are the prize for this community, they are specifically targeting our children."[40]

During this campaign Bachmann repeatedly exhibited a homophobic bigotry unrivalled by any of her fellow Republican candidates. For example, during a radio interview she charged that if the amendment did not pass, public school students "will be required to learn that homosexuality is normal, equal, and perhaps you should try it."[41] Shortly thereafter, she repeated this same theme: "And what a bizarre time we're in . . . when a judge will say to little children that you can't say the pledge of allegiance, but you must learn that homosexuality is normal and you should try it." And again on yet another radio program: "Our children will be forced to learn that homosexuality is normal and natural and that perhaps they should try it, and that'll be very soon in our public schools all across the state, beginning in kindergarten."[42] How many crimes of violence against gays and lesbians may have resulted from this public gay bashing cannot be known, but Bachmann has never apologized for this hateful ranting.

Her nuttiness, in fact, seems to know no bounds. Like so many other religious extremists, she loves to blame natural disasters on groups and individuals she hates. After Hurricane Irene inflicted so much damage on the East Coast in August 2011, then was followed by an earthquake that same month that rattled citizens up and down the East Coast, Bachmann stated to a group of seniors in Florida, "I don't know how much God has to do to get our attention of the politicians. . . . We've had an earthquake; we've had a hurricane. He said, 'Are you going to start listening to me here? Listen to the American people because the American people are roaring right now.'"[43] If nothing else, Bachmann should be congratulated on her campaign prowess: having God himself as your campaign manager is certainly no small feat.

It comes as no surprise, then, that she is uniformly opposed to granting gays and lesbians full legal equality. Despite touting herself as a supporter of the Tenth Amendment, as so many Tea Party activists do, she supports the federalization of marriage by passing a federal marriage amendment to the US Constitution and strictly enforcing DOMA.[44] She has stated several times that she will attempt to reverse the repeal of DADT,[45] and she opposes any kind of employment protection for gay and lesbian employees, even in the public sector. Although she protested several times during the nomination process that she does not hate gays and lesbians and that she would have considered appointing an openly gay person to her administration, her long record of opposition to gay rights, together with the hateful language she repeatedly used when referring to gay Americans, calls her honesty into question.

Rating: F

RON PAUL

Representative Ron Paul has been (and continues to be) the single most visible agent of change in the Republican Party during the past four years, and he was also one of the founders of the early Tea Party movement. His long history of libertarian activism, both within and outside the Republican Party, went largely unnoticed outside the libertarian movement until his first run for the Republican nomination for president in 2007. Although he developed an avid, almost fanatical following during that campaign, he won no primaries and was not considered a serious contender simply because of his admittedly radical views, not just on fiscal and economic issues but also in foreign affairs and social issues.

Paul's fundamental libertarian philosophy is a pretty good predictor of where he comes down on gay and lesbian issues, but it's not a slam dunk. When asked at the Values Voters Presidential Debate sponsored by a coalition of Religious Right organizations on September 17, 2007, "What do you intend to do to counteract the homosexual agenda?" Paul responded, "If you want to change people, you change them through persuasion, through family values and church values, but you can't do it through legislation because force doesn't work. But if homosexual groups want to enforce their way on us, there's no right to do that either. At the same time, you should eradicate all these hate [crime] laws. They indicate that some people would receive a different penalty than others."[46] Most Christian evangelicals, of course, believe that government should actively promote their religious values, a kind of social engineering of the Right, but that view is fundamentally opposed to the live-and-let-live beliefs of Paul and other libertarians.

Representative Paul has stated many times that the state should not be involved in marriage: "My personal belief is that marriage is a religious ceremony. And it should be dealt with religiously. The [government] shouldn't be involved."[47] He believes marriage is and should be a state issue and has long opposed the Federal Marriage Amendment,[48] but he seems confused about the Defense of Marriage Act and what it actually does.[49] While repeatedly saying the federal government should not define what marriage is, he has expressed support for the measure, seemingly oblivious of the fact that Section 3 of the law clearly interferes with the Tenth Amendment right of each state to define marriage for itself. Paul has stated that he supports DOMA[50] as a defensive measure because it prevents the federal government from forcing individual states to recognize same-sex marriages performed in other states because of the Full Faith and Credit Clause of the Constitution. Indeed, Section 2 does do that, but it goes much further. Retaining Section 2 may arguably be an option worth considering, but clearly Section 3 directly violates Paul's own belief in the Tenth Amendment and should be repealed.

Paul has been a consistent opponent of the DADT policy and was among a handful of congressional Republicans (one of fifteen) voting to repeal it,[51] and he has been denounced for that vote by a variety of right-wing pundits. He opposes the federal Employment Non-Discrimination Act (ENDA) as well as adding sexual orientation to the federal hate crime statute,[52] but it's important to note that he opposes those bills for *any* group as an unconstitutional violation of private property and local law enforcement, respectively.

A Paul presidency would likely be a step forward for expanding relationship recognition for gay and lesbian couples across the states, but until he changes his position on DOMA by supporting either narrowing it or repealing it, his consistent commitment to the principles he espouses must be questioned.

Rating: C

HERMAN CAIN

Because Cain never held elective office, few took his presidential campaign seriously. He provided some moments of well-stated critiques of President Barack Obama's economic agenda during the campaign. Unfortunately, he also followed the usual anti-gay playbook of the Far Right and even earned the approval of the AFA's Bryan Fischer, its overtly homophobic spokesman, after having appeared on his show several times.[53]

Cain opposes not just same-sex marriage but also civil unions.[54] Although early in the campaign he said he was opposed to the Federal Marriage Amendment, he subsequently stated his support for it;[55] he is also an enthusiastic supporter of DOMA.[56] He castigated President Obama for his decision to decline to defend DOMA in court against the numerous lawsuits that have been filed against it, labeling his refusal "treason."[57]

Although he earned the condemnation of the National Organization for Marriage for his initial refusal to sign its marriage pledge—something that Bachmann, Santorum, Romney, and Perry were all too happy to do—it had little to do with any substantive disagreement with what the pledge demanded.

Cain publicly stated he would consider hiring openly gay applicants for jobs in his administration and yet tried to cover up the fact that one of his top advisors and the treasurer of his political action committee was gay after his campaign tried to ease the aide out quietly due to objections from some of Cain's supporters.[58]

Unlike many of the other Republican candidates, Cain initially declined to say he would work to repeal DADT, stating in a New Hampshire primary debate in June 2011, "I would not create a distraction trying to overturn it as president,"[59] but he later reversed his position on that as well.

Ultimately, Cain will probably become little more than an interesting footnote to the 2012 presidential campaign, and given his open embrace of most of the usual anti-gay agenda, that will not be an unfortunate outcome.

Rating: D–

RICK SANTORUM

At the beginning of the Republican presidential nominating process, it appeared that former senator Rick Santorum from Pennsylvania would be staking out the most anti-gay reputation of all the candidates, so he must have been sorely disappointed at the emergence of Representative Bachmann and Governor Perry as serious contenders for the nomination, both of whom have gone head-to-head with him to win the hearts and minds of the most anti-gay elements of the party.

As far back as 2003, when the US Supreme Court declared the remaining state sodomy laws unconstitutional, Rick Santorum condemned the decision, saying, "If you have the right to consensual sex within your home, then you have the right to bigamy, you have the right to incest, you have the right to adultery. You have the right to anything."[60] He has been a consistent critic of libertarianism, condemning it for its emphasis on the rights of individuals versus the state.[61]

In the Senate, he voted at least twice against adding sexual orientation to the hate crime statute,[62] which covers racial, religious, and ethnic bias. He voted against adding sexual orientation to the federal employment nondiscrimination statute,[63] not out of any principled objection to federal regulation of private employers but merely because he doesn't believe gay people are worthy of being protected. He voted for the Federal Marriage Amendment in 2006[64] and opposes all relationship recognition for gay couples. He supports the continuation of DOMA,[65] and he stated in the June 2011 Republican candidates' debate in New Hampshire that he would work to resurrect DADT.[66]

His outspoken anti-gay record no doubt played a part in his overwhelming defeat for reelection to the Senate in 2006, and his views on gay and lesbian issues are today outside the mainstream of American voters, including Republicans.

Rating: F

TIM PAWLENTY

Shortly after Governor Pawlenty entered office in Minnesota in 2003, he supported a bill that extended nondiscrimination protections to gays and lesbians in the areas of housing, employment, education, and public accommodations.[67] That was one of the very few times he supported gay rights, and he later expressed regret for supporting the bill since it covered gender identity as well as sexual orientation.[68]

In 1997, while still governor, he supported a state ban on same-sex marriage, and he has reiterated that view many times since, arguing that "opposite-sex marriage is the cornerstone of our society" and that it should "be elevated . . . to a special level." In 2003, he argued that a proposed state amendment to ban gay marriage was unnecessary, but under relentless pressure from then state senator Michele Bachmann and others, he endorsed the amendment, which passed in 2004.[69] That same year, to his credit, he refused to sign a bill that would have repealed the 1993 Human Rights Act.[70] His spokesman stated at the time that "this law is not about gay rights or 'special rights'—it is about human rights and fairness for all."[71] That was the last time Pawlenty ever spoke in favor of gay rights.

In 2010, Governor Pawlenty vetoed a state bill that would have given gays and lesbians the right to decide what to do with the body of their deceased partner, arguing that it was unnecessary since they could hire a lawyer and draw up a living will.[72] That hateful act served him well in trying to placate the anti-gay Right in building up to announcing his candidacy for president. He put little daylight between himself and most of the other Republican presidential candidates on gay issues, losing whatever appeal he might have once had to political moderates and independents in a general election.

In 2011, Pawlenty signed NOM's marriage pledge and took every opportunity to express his views opposing gay rights and any support for relationship recognition for gay couples.[73] He pledged several times to try to overturn the repeal of DADT[74] and promised to enforce DOMA to whatever extent possible.[75]

Despite his repeated attempts to portray himself as every bit as anti-gay as he needed to be to win the Republican nomination, he apparently wasn't authentic enough for the hard Right voters he was courting, and on August 14, 2011, after a dismal third-place showing in the Iowa Straw Poll, he withdrew from the race. He subsequently endorsed Governor Romney for the nomination.

Rating: D–

NEWT GINGRICH

It's no doubt difficult for millions of Americans to understand how former Speaker of the House Newt Gingrich can, after having divorced twice and now being married to his third wife, reinvent himself as a spokesman for traditional marriage and family values, but this is America.

Anything is possible, and, as of this writing, Gingrich's presidential quest is going well, especially with the anti-gay Republican voters whom he is so feverishly courting.

Gingrich has been doing whatever he can for many years to kill any expansion of rights for gay and lesbian Americans, and he reiterated that opposition in 2011 with an appearance on rabidly anti-gay Bryan Fischer's radio show, pledging that, if elected president, he will do whatever he can to slow down the progress of gay rights[76]: "I think my emphasis would be pro-classical Christianity,"[77] he told Fischer, although he presumably does not include biblical calls for the killing of adulterers in his definition of Christianity.

Gingrich helped sponsor and pass DOMA[78] when it was first proposed by President Bill Clinton, and he called for the impeachment of President Obama when his administration decided it would no longer defend DOMA[79] in the courts, even though it will continue to enforce the law while it is on the books. He has long supported the Federal Marriage Amendment[80] and opposed any kind of relationship recognition for gay and lesbian couples.

He joined the right-wing chorus calling for keeping DADT[81] and ultimately signed NOM's marriage pledge.[82] In an attempt to win over evangelicals in Iowa, he bankrolled the campaign to remove three Iowa judges who had ruled the state's prohibition on same-sex marriage unconstitutional.[83] That campaign was successful, and the same activists who were behind it launched an effort to pass a state constitutional amendment in 2012 to end Iowa's status as one of just seven states where gays and lesbians can legally marry. That effort failed, and the amendment will not appear on the ballot.

Gingrich has used his run for the White House to solidify his legacy as a leader in the movement to squash gay rights, just as the nation continues a dramatic move in the opposite direction.

Rating: F

JON HUNTSMAN

Former governor of Utah and ambassador to China Jon Huntsman has a sterling resume and movie-star good looks, and yet he remained unknown to most Republican primary voters. That was unfortunate, because he was one of the few Republican candidates in this election cycle whose views on gay rights are solidly in sync with not just independent voters but the Republican rank and file as well.

As governor, Huntsman signed legislation in 2008 expanding domestic partner benefits for Utah's unmarried couples, both gay and straight,[84] and he has been a consistent supporter of civil unions and other measures like hospital visitation rights for same-sex partners,[85] even though these measures never passed the state legislature. Huntsman has never backed away from his support for expanding gay rights such as civil unions, infuriating the anti-gay lobby but reflecting the views of mainstream America.

As a true federalist, he opposes the Federal Marriage Amendment[86] and other federal attempts to tell the states what to do on this issue, and he supported the end of DADT,[87] like the great majority of voters. He refused to sign NOM's Marriage Vow.[88]

Because of his socially tolerant views on gay rights, of course, some on the right fling the term "RINO" (Republican in Name Only) at him, and yet even a superficial look at a wide range of his views shows how inaccurate that silly term is when applied to Huntsman. He was one of the strongest pro-life candidates in the field; he had a solid conservative record as governor; he supports a balanced budget amendment to the US Constitution; and he is a strong supporter of gun rights, having expanded the rights of gun owners when he was governor. He combines a strong fiscal conservatism with a modern and appealing sense of social tolerance that would have made him a very strong candidate in the general election.

Rating: B–

GARY JOHNSON

A former two-term governor of New Mexico, Gary Johnson was, until his withdrawal in late 2011, the most libertarian candidate in the race besides Ron Paul. He was also the most outspoken candidate in favor of gay rights, making him a candidate who would have had wide appeal on both the left and right sides of the political spectrum. Unfortunately, because Johnson has had low poll numbers, he was not included in most of the debates of Republican candidates, the usual catch-22 situation in which candidates who are not well enough known are excluded precisely because they are not included in the debates.

Johnson made his views regarding social tolerance and individual rights known when he and the other candidates were asked to sign an anti–gay marriage pledge put forth by an Iowa religious organization called The Family Leader in the summer of 2011. The pledge asked the candidates to "vigorously" oppose gay marriage, pornography, and Islamic "sharia law," as well as to defend DOMA, reverse the repeal of DADT, support the Federal Marriage Amendment, and submit to a variety of other social and economic demands, swearing allegiance to the pledge in the name of God.

Johnson wasted no time denouncing the Marriage Vow, as it was called, as "offensive to the principles of liberty and freedom on which this country was founded."[89] "The Republican Party cannot be sidetracked into discussing these morally judgmental issues," he continued, concluding that "the pledge is nothing short of a promise to discriminate against everyone who makes a personal choice that doesn't fit into a particular definition of 'virtue.'" Even socially conservative candidates like Cain, Gingrich, Romney, and Pawlenty refused to sign it, as did Representative Paul.

Governor Johnson announced his support for marriage equality in late 2011,[90] opposes DOMA and the Federal Marriage Amendment,[91] and applauded the end of DADT.[92] His one-time presence in the Republican field, along with that of Huntsman and Paul, gives hope that Republicans will not allow their party to continue to be steered on social issues by organizations and individuals who represent a small slice of American voters.

Rating: A

Most Americans are intensely focused on economic issues right now and remain dissatisfied with Obama's stewardship of the economy. They are also finally waking up to the enormous challenges we face in reforming entitlements and paying off our huge national debt. Understandably, social issues like expanding legal rights for gay and lesbian Americans may take a back seat to getting our fiscal house in order, and even voters who support gay rights may opt to support a candidate with whom they disagree about gay rights in order to right our economic ship of state. On the other hand, supporting a candidate who is right on economic issues but wrong on social tolerance may be too much to bear for many independents and libertarians who personally value equality and individual freedom. It will be a tough choice for millions of Americans, but one thing is clear: support for gay rights is wide, deep, and growing. Anti-gay bigotry is dying, and Republicans, conservatives, and libertarians must help bury it once and for all.

NOTES

PREFACE

1. See, for example, Claremont Institute, "Not Your Father's Republican Party," www.claremont.org/publications/pub_print.asp?pubid=456; Sara Diamond, "On the Road to Political Power and Theocracy," Political Research Associates, www.publiceye.org/eyes/sd_theo.html.

2. See "Christian Right," Wikipedia, http://en.wikipedia.org/wiki/Christian_right.

3. Ibid.

4. Ibid.

5. Claremont Institute, "Not Your Father's Republican Party."

6. See Wikipedia, "Christian Right."

7. Pat Buchanan, "1992 Republican National Convention Speech," Wikipedia, August 17, 1992, http://en.wikipedia.org/wiki/Pat_Buchanan.

8. "Big Scary List of Pat Buchanan Quotes," Positive Atheism, October 15, 2000, www.positiveatheism.org/hist/quotes/buchanan.htm.

9. Scott Keeter, "Will White Evangelicals Desert the GOP?" Pew Research Center, May 2, 2006, http://pewresearch.org/pubs/22/will-white-evangelicals-desert-the-gop.

10. Ibid.

11. Ibid.

12. See, for example, "Democratic Party Platform and Republican Party Platform on Equality," eQualityGiving, 2008, www.equalitygiving.org/party-platform.

13. Howard Phillips, "President Bush and the Homosexual Activist Agenda," DutyIsOurs, http://dutyisours.com/50+h.htm.

14. See "Federal Marriage Amendment," Wikipedia, http://en.wikipedia.org/wiki/Federal_Marriage_Amendment.

15. David Boaz, "The Ohio 'Values Voters' Myth, Again," Cato@Liberty, October 11, 2006, www.Cato-at-liberty.org/the-ohio-values-voters-myth-again.

16. Ibid.

17. "Fewer Voters Identify as Republicans," Pew Research Organization, March 20, 2008, http://pewresearch.org/pubs/773/fewer-voters-identify-as-republicans.

18. eQualityGiving, "Democratic Party Platform and Republican Party Platform on Equality."

19. Vic Gold, *Invasion of the Party Snatchers: How the Holy-Rollers and Neo-Cons Destroyed the GOP* (Naperville, IL: Sourcebooks, 2007).

20. Maggie Haberman, "Ralph Reed: Social Issues Up Front," *Politico*, March 7, 2011, www.politico.com/news/stories/0311/50763.html.

21. Ibid.

22. "GOP Contenders Make Early Pitch to Iowa Evangelicals," CNN.com, March 9, 2011, http://articles.cnn.com/2011-03-08/politics/iowa.gop_1_potential-candidates-social-conservatives-santorum/2?_s=PM:POLITICS.

23. Brian Montopoli, "Rick Santorum Returns—and Eyes the White House," CBSNews.com, April 21, 2010, www.cbsnews.com/stories/2010/04/20/politics/main6415666.shtml.

24. Eric W. Dolan, "Four Republican Presidential Candidates Sign NOM Marriage Pledge," Raw Story, August 7, 2011, www.rawstory.com/rs/2011/08/07/four-republican-presidential-candidates-sign-nom-marriage-pledge.

25. See "Republican Party (United States)," Wikipedia, http://en.wikipedia.org/wiki/Republican_Party_(United_States).

26. Ibid.

27. Ibid.

28. Karen Ocamb, "Will LGBT Progressives Work with Log Cabin Republicans in 2011," LGBT | POV, December 27, 2010, www.lgbtpov.com/2010/12/will-lgbt-progressives-work-with-log-cabin-republicans-in-2011.

29. "42 Percent of Americans Live in States that Recognize Gay Unions," *On Top Magazine*, March 28, 2011, www.ontopmag.com/article.aspx?id=7940&MediaType=1&Category=26.

30. Amy Gardner, "Gauging the Scope of the Tea Party Movement in America," *Washington Post*, October 24, 2010, A9.

31. See CNN/*Time* Poll, October 14–15, 1998, at "Law and Civil Rights," Polling Report, www.pollingreport.com/civil.htm; *Newsweek* Poll, December 4–5, 2008, at Polling Report, "Law and Civil Rights"; CBS News Poll, August 20–24, 2010, at Polling Report, "Law and Civil Rights"; Lymari Morales, "Conservatives Shift in Favor of Openly Gay Service Members," Gallup, June 5,

2009, www.gallup.com/poll/120764/Conservatives-Shift-Favor-Openly-Gay-Service-Members.aspx.

CHAPTER 1: A SHORT HISTORY OF THE GAY RIGHTS MOVEMENT

1. Dudly Clendinen and Adam Nagourney, *Out for Good* (New York: Simon & Schuster, 1999), 12.

2. See, for example, Jonathan Katz, *Gay American History: Lesbians and Gay Men in the U.S.A.* (New York: Thomas Y. Crowell, 1976).

3. Ibid.

4. Ibid.

5. Ibid.

6. David Carter, *Stonewall: The Riots that Sparked the Gay Revolution* (New York: St. Martin's Press, 2004).

7. Jonathan Katz, *Gay American History*.

8. David Carter, *Stonewall: The Riots that Sparked the Gay Revolution*, 15.

9. Ibid.

10. Ibid.

11. U.S. Government Executive Order 10450, "Security Requirements for Government Employees," 1953.

12. Kenneth S. Wherry, "Report of the Investigations of the Junior Senator of Nebraska, a Member of the Subcommittee Appointed by the Subcommittee on Appropriations for the District of Columbia, on the Infiltration of Subversives and Moral Perverts into the Executive Branch of the United States Government," 1950.

13. David Carter, *Stonewall: The Riots that Sparked the Gay Revolution*.

14. Ibid.

15. Ibid.

16. Jonathan Katz, *Gay American History*.

17. Ibid.

18. See "LGBT Rights in the United States," Wikipedia, http://wikipedia.org/wiki/LGBT_rights_in_the_United_States.

19. David Carter, *Stonewall: The Riots that Sparked the Gay Revolution*.

20. Ibid.

21. See "Stonewall Riots," Wikipedia, http://en.wikipedia.org/wiki/Stonewall_riots.

22. Jonathan Katz, *Gay American History*.

23. William N. Eskridge Jr., "Why Americans Will Accept Gay Troops before They Accept Gay Marriage," *Washington Post*, December 3, 2010.

24. Nikki Finke, "GLAAD Study: Number of LGBT Characters Up for 2010–2011 Broadcast TV Season," Deadline, September 29, 2010, www.deadline.com/2010/09/glaad-study-number-of-lgbt-characters-up-for-2010-2011-broadcast-tv-season.

25. Roy Childs, editorial, *Libertarian Review*, July 1977.

26. Martin Duberman, *Stonewall* (New York: Penguin Books, 1993).

27. Bryan Bender, "Gays Being Kicked Out of Military at Steady Rate," *Boston Globe*, May 19, 2009, www.boston.com/news/politics/politicalintelligence/2009/05/gays_being_kick.html.

28. Wikipedia, "LGBT Rights in the United States."

29. See "Executive Order 13087," Wikipedia, http://en.wikipedia.org/wiki/Executive_Order_13087.

30. See "The American Gay Rights Movement: A Timeline," InfoPlease, http://infoplease.com/ipa/A0761909.html.

31. Ibid.

32. See "Federal Marriage Amendment," Wikipedia, http://en.wikipedia.org/wiki/Federal_Marriage_Amendment.

33. Ibid.

CHAPTER 2: WHY THE RELIGIOUS RIGHT IS WRONG ABOUT THE SEPARATION OF CHURCH AND STATE

1. "Jefferson's Letter to the Danbury Baptists," Library of Congress, January 1, 1802, www.loc.gov/loc/lcib/9806/danpre.html.

2. Quoted in *Ms.* magazine, February 1987; see "Quotes from Beverly LaHaye," at "Concerned Women for America," Right Wing Watch, www.rightwingwatch.org/print/2579.

3. Ibid.

4. Russell Shorto, "How Christian Were the Founders?" *New York Times*, February 2, 2010, www.nytimes.com/2010/02/14/magazine/14texbooks-t.html.

5. Frank Lambert, *Religion in American Politics: A Short History* (Princeton, NJ: Princeton University Press, 2008).

6. See "The Pocket Constitution," U.S. Constitution Online, www.usconstitution.net/tripoli.html.

7. Isaac Kramnick and R. Laurence Moore, *The Godless Constitution* (New York: W. W. Norton, 2005).

8. Russell Shorto, "How Christian Were the Founders?"

9. Paul F. Boller, *George Washington and Religion* (Dallas, TX: Southern Methodist University Press, 1963).

10. See "Our Founding Fathers Were Not Christians," July 2011, http://freethought.mbdojo.com/foundingfathers.html.

11. Robert S. Alley, ed., *James Madison on Religious Liberty* (Amherst, NY: Prometheus Books, 1989).

12. See "James Madison," Wikiquote, http://en.wikiquote.org/wiki/James_Madison.

13. See "Our Founding Fathers Were Not Christians."

14. Ibid.

15. Ibid.

16. See "Superstition of Christianity," Thomas Jefferson's Monticello, www.monticello.org/site/jefferson/superstition-christianity-quotation-0.

17. See "Our Founding Fathers Were Not Christians."

18. See "Quotes," Early American History, www.earlyamericanhistory.net/quotes.htm.

19. See "Our Founding Fathers Were Not Christians."

20. *American Heritage Dictionary*, 4th ed. (Boston: Houghton Mifflin, 2006).

21. E. J. Dionne, "The New Republic: Mark Souder, You Broke My Heart," NPR, May 24, 2010, www.npr.org/templates/story/story.php?storyId=127086343.

22. "Faith in Egypt: Excerpts from On Faith," *Washington Post*, February 5, 2011.

23. See "Santorum: 'America Belongs to God,'" a speech before the 2011 Conservative Political Action Conference, Right Wing Watch, February 10, 2011, www.rightwingwatch.org/content/santorum-america-belong-god.

24. Senator Sam Brownback, fund-raising letter to supporters, 2007.

25. "Inside Ronald Reagan," an interview with Ronald Reagan, *Reason*, July 1, 1975.

26. Goldwater never labeled himself a libertarian, but his pro-choice, pro-gay rights views set him distinctly apart from the Religious Right, which he criticized repeatedly during his Senate career. See "A Profile of Barry Goldwater," About.com, http://usconservatives.about.com/od/conservativepolitics101/a/GoldwaterProfil.htm.

27. *Anderson Cooper 360 Degrees*, "Jerry Falwell's Legacy," CNN.com, May 15, 2007, http://transcripts.cnn.com/TRANSCRIPTS/0705/15/acd.01.html.

28. See the Libertarian Christians website (www.libertarianchristians.com).

29. Doug Bandow, *Beyond Good Intentions: A Biblical View of Politics* (Wheaton, IL: Crossways, 1999).

30. Claremont Institute, "Not Your Father's Republican Party," www.claremont.org/publications/pub_print.asp?pubid=456.

31. Sara Diamond, "On the Road to Political Power and Theocracy," Political Research Associates, 2010, www.publiceye.org/eyes/sd_theo.html.

32. "Stupid, Scary and Ignorant Quotes," ExChristian.net, http://articles.exchristian.net/2003/11/stupid-scary-and-ignorant-quotes.php.

33. Ibid.

34. Scott Keeter, "Will White Evangelicals Desert the GOP?" Pew Research Center, May 2, 2006, www.pewtrusts.org/news_room_detail.aspx?id=23850.

35. See "How Groups Voted in 1984," Roper Center, www.ropercenter.uconn.edu/elections/how_groups_voted/voted_84.html.

36. See "How Groups Voted in 1988," Roper Center, www.ropercenter.uconn.edu/elections/how_groups_voted/voted_88.html.

37. See "How Groups Voted in 1996," Roper Center, www.ropercenter.uconn.edu/elections/how_groups_voted/voted_96.html.

38. See "How Groups Voted in 2008," Roper Center, www.ropercenter.uconn.edu/elections/how_groups_voted/voted_08.html.

39. See "How Groups Voted in 1980," Roper Center, www.ropercenter.uconn.edu/elections/how_groups_voted/voted_80.html.

40. See Roper Center, "How Groups Voted in 1984."

41. See Roper Center, "How Groups Voted in 1988."

42. See Roper Center, "How Groups Voted in 2008."

43. See Roper Center, "How Groups Voted in 1980."

44. See Roper Center, "How Groups Voted in 1988."

45. See Roper Center, "How Groups Voted in 2008."

46. See Roper Center, "How Groups Voted in 1984."

47. See Roper Center, "How Groups Voted in 2008."

48. See Roper Center, "How Groups Voted in 1984."

49. See Roper Center, "How Groups Voted in 2008."

50. Statement on October 6, 1935; see William J. Federer, "FDR: Like the Bible, the Constitution Should Be Re-Read Consistantly," Moral Liberal, January 30, 2011, www.themoralliberal.com/2011/01/30/fdr-like-the-bible-the-constitution-should-be-re-read-consistantly.

51. Marilyn Gardner, "Anti-SUV Query: 'What Would Jesus Drive?'" *Christian Science Monitor*, http://archive.glennbeck.com/jesus/whatwouldjesusdrive.shtml.

52. "Invoking Tea Party Anger, Thousands Rally in D.C. in Support of Dems' Agenda," FoxNews.com, October 2, 2010, www.foxnews.com/politics/2010/10/02/labor-civil-rights-groups-rally-washington.

53. Krissah Thompson and Spencer Hsu, "Tens of Thousands Attend Progressive 'One Nation Working Together' Rally in Washington," *Washington Post*, October 2, 2010.

54. Dan Gilgoff, "New Budget Campaign Asks, 'What Would Jesus Cut?'" *CNN Belief Blog*, February 28, 2011, www.washingtonpost.com/wp-dyn/content/article/2010/10/01/AR201010 0104440_pf.html.

55. Marie Diamond, "'What Would Jesus Cut?' Christian Leaders Urge Obama to Protect the Poor in Debt Talks," Think Progress, July 27, 2011, http://thinkprogress.org/economy/2011/07/27/280361/what-would-jesus-cut.

56. John Amato, "Ayn Rand & GOP vs Jesus," Crooks and Liars, June 9, 2011, http://crooksandliars.com/node/47065/print.

57. Mark Tooley, "Choosing Ayn Rand or Jesus?" *American Spectator*, June 6, 2011, http://spectator.org/archives/2011/06/07/ayn-rand-and-karl-marx.

58. See "Christians Must Choose: Ayn Rand or Jesus," American Values Network, http://americanvaluesnetwork.org/aynrandvsjesus.

59. Ibid.

60. Sheryl Gay Stolberg, "Obama Talks about His Faith," *New York Times*, Caucus, September 28, 2010, http://thecaucus.blogs.nytimes.com/2010/09/28/obama-talks-about-his-faith-2.

61. Peter Hamby, "Obama: GOP Doesn't Own Faith Issue," CNN.com, October 8, 2007, http://articles.cnn.com/2007-10-08/politics/obama.faith_1_obama-s-south-carolina-rick-warren-faith?_s=PM:POLITICS.

62. Albert Mohler, "Divorce—the Scandal of the Evangelical Conscience," Christian Worldview, September 30, 2010, http://thechristianworldview.com/tcwblog/archives/4249.

63. Mark A. Smith, "Religion, Divorce, and the Missing Culture War in America," *Political Science Quarterly* 125, no. 1 (spring 2010).

64. David Gibson, "Conservative Christians Tackle Divorce, the 'Other' Marriage Crisis," Politics Daily, October 3, 2010, www.politicsdaily.com/2010/10/03/conservative-christians-tackle-divorce-the-other-marriage-cri.

65. Ibid.

66. Albert Mohler, "Divorce—The Scandal of the Evangelical Conscience."

67. David Gibson, "Conservative Christians Tackle Divorce, the 'Other' Marriage Crisis."

68. Ibid.

CHAPTER 3: WHAT ARE GAY RIGHTS?

1. David Carter, *Stonewall: The Riots that Sparked the Gay Revolution* (New York: St. Martin's Press, 2004); Jonathan Katz, *Gay American History: Lesbians and Gay Men in the U.S.A.* (New York: Thomas Y. Crowell, 1976).

2. Ibid.

3. Ibid.

4. See "Employment Non-Discrimination Act," Wikipedia, http://en.wikipedia.org/wiki/Employment_Non-Discrimination_Act.

5. Ibid.

6. Dale Carpenter, "An ENDA Thanksgiving," Independent Gay Forum, November 22, 2007, http://igfculturewatch.com/2007/11/22/an-enda-thanksgiving.

7. See Wikipedia, "Employment Non-Discrimination Act."

8. See "Barney Frank and Activists Dig In Their Heels over ENDA," Towleroad, October 12, 2007, www.towleroad.com/2007/10/barney-frank-an/comments/page/1.

9. See Wikipedia, "Employment Non-Discrimination Act."

10. See a variety of polls at "Law and Civil Rights," Polling Report, www.pollingreport.com/civil.htm; see also "Public Opinion Polls: 1995–2001," Religious Tolerance, www.religioustolerance.org/hom_empl10.htm.

11. Ibid.

12. Ibid.

13. Ibid.

14. See Religious Tolerance, "Public Opinion Polls: 1995–2001."

15. Ibid.

16. See Religious Tolerance, "Public Opinion Polls: 1995–2001."

17. See Jeff Krehely, "Polls Show Huge Public Support for Gay and Transgender Workplace Protections," Center for American Progress, June 2, 2011, www.americanprogress.org/issues/2011/06/protection_poll.html.

18. "Domestic Partner Benefits: Facts and Background," Employee Benefit Research Institute, February 2009.

19. See www.hrc.org/resources/entry/corporate-equality-index-2011.

20. For an interesting discussion of antidiscrimination laws from a libertarian perspective, see David Bernstein, "Context Matters: A Better Libertarian Approach to Antidiscrimination Law," Cato Unbound, June 16, 2010, www.guardian.co.uk/commentisfree/2008/feb/29/sexreligionandconservatives/print.

21. See, for example, the websites of two extreme anti-gay organizations, the Family Research Council (www.frc.org) and the American Family Association (www.afa.net).

22. For a list of this and other pro-gay actions by President Bush, see "Christian Concerned Women of America," Cutting Edge, www.cuttingedge.org/news/n1652.cfm. Opponents and supporters of President Bush were surprised by these actions.

23. See "Domestic Partners Benefits and Obligations Act," Log Cabin, www.logcabin.org/site/c.nsKSL7PMLpF/b.6417753/k.6424/Domestic_Partners_Benefits_and_Obligations_Act.htm.

24. Lisa Rein, "Same-Sex Partners' Benefits Lag," *Washington Post*, November 18, 2010.

25. Ibid.

26. See Polling Report, "Law and Civil Rights."

27. Ibid.

28. Chris Johnson, "McDermott Introduces Pro-Gay Tax Equity Bill," *Washington Blade*, June 9, 2011, www.washingtonblade.com/2011/06/09/mcdermott-introduces-pro-gay-tax-equity-bill.

29. See "Unequal Taxes on Equal Benefits: The Taxation of Domestic Partner Benefits," Center for American Progress, December 3, 2007, www.americanprogress.org/events/2007/12/costequality.html.

30. David Kopel, "Hate Crime Laws Dangerous and Divisive," Independence Institute, Issue Paper No. 3-2003, January 13, 2003.

31. See www.fbi.gov/about-us/cjis/ucr/hate-crime/2010/index.

32. Janet Smith, "Anti-Gay Hate Crimes: Doing the Math," Southern Poverty Law Center, *Intelligence Report* No. 140 (Winter 2010), www.splcenter.org/get-informed/intelligence-report/browse-all-issues/2010/winter/anti-gay-hate-crimes-doing-the-math.

33. Ibid.

34. Ibid.

35. Ibid.

36. See ThinkExist.com, "Barry Goldwater Quotes," http://thinkexist.com/quotation/you_don-t_have_to_be_straight_to_be_in_the/200248.html.

37. "Retired Military Officials: Repeal Ban, Let Gays Serve Openly," *USA Today*, November 17, 2008.

38. Associated Press, "Tough for Gay Members to Return to Full Military," FoxNews.com, August 13, 2011, www.foxnews.com/us/2011/08/13/tough-for-gay-members-to-return-to-full-military-865048271.

39. Ed O'Keefe, "Replacing Openly Gay Troops Cost Pentagon $193 Million over 6 Years," *Washington Post*, January 21, 2011.

40. Ibid.

41. "Opinions of Military Personnel on Sexual Minorities in the Military," Zogby International Poll, December 2006, www.palmcenter.org/files/active/1/ZogbyReport.pdf.

42. Ibid.

43. Ibid.

44. Ibid.

45. Greg Zoroya, "Pentagon Study Backs End to 'Don't Ask, Don't Tell,'" *USA Today*, December 1, 2010, www.usatoday.com/news/military/2010-11-30-study-gay-military-service_N.htm.

46. Ibid.

47. Ibid.

48. General James Amos, 35th Commandant of the Marine Corps, "Statement on the Repeal of Title 10, U.S. Code 654 'Policy Concerning Homosexuality in the United States Armed Forces' (Don't Ask, Don't Tell)," December 19, 2010.

49. See "Sexual Orientation and Military Service," Wikipedia, http://en.wikipedia.org/wiki/Sexual_orientation_and_military_service.

50. Ibid.

51. For a variety of polls on DADT, see Polling Report, "Law and Civil Rights."

52. Ibid.

53. Ibid.

54. Ibid.

55. Ibid.

56. Ibid.

57. Jessica Brandy, "Senate Passes 'Don't Ask, Don't Tell' Repeal," *Roll Call*, December 18, 2010, www.rollcall.com/news/-201638-1.html.

58. Ibid.

59. Neal Broverman, "DADT Lawsuit Not Dead Yet," Advocate.com, December 22, 2010, www.advocate.com/News/Daily_News/2010/12/22/DADT_Lawsuit_Not_Dead_Yet.

60. Brief for Cato Institute as Amicus Curiae Supporting Petitioners, *Lawrence v. Texas*, 539 U.S. 558 (2003) (No. 02-102).

61. See Randy E. Barnett, "Justice Kennedy's Libertarian Revolution: *Lawrence v. Texas*," in *Cato Supreme Court Review*, edited by Ilya Shapiro (Washington, DC: Cato Institute, 2003).

62. Stuart Shepard, "Supreme Court Considers Texas Sodomy Law," Focus on the Family, March 27, 2003.

63. Ibid.

64. Frank Newport, "Six Out of 10 Americans Say Homosexual Relations Should Be Recognized as Legal," Gallup News Service, May 15, 2003, www.gallup.com/poll/8413/six-americans-say-homosexual-relations-should-recognized-legal.aspx.

65. Ibid.

66. Harris Interactive Poll, "Seven in Ten Adult Americans Support U.S. Supreme Court Overturning Same-Sex Sodomy Laws," Harris Interactive, May 6, 2003, www.harrisinteractive.com/news/allnewsbydate.asp?NewsID=616.

67. Ibid.

68. See, for example, Bryan Fischer from the American Family Association calling for reinstituting state sodomy laws: Brian Tashman "Fischer: Make Homosexuality 'A Criminal Offense,'" Right Wing Watch, August 30, 2011, www.rightwingwatch.org/content/fischer-make-homosexuality-criminal-offense.

69. Tim Murphy, "The Unconstitutional Anti-Gay Law that Just Won't Die," *Mother Jones*, April 13, 2011, http://motherjones.com/politics/2011/04/lawrence-texas-homosexual-conduct-statute.

70. Ibid.

71. See Appendix 4: Categories of Statutory Provisions, GAO-04-353R Defense of Marriage Act, 16.

72. "Gay and Lesbian Couples Pay Thousands More in Taxes, Study Says," *Huffington Post*, December 28, 2011.

73. "Bereaved Spouse Challenges 'DOMA' as Unconstitutional" (news release), American Civil Liberties Union, November 8, 2010.

74. Ibid.

75. See "Challenging Federal Marriage Discrimination," Gay & Lesbian Advocates and Defenders, www.glad.org/doma/faq-pedersen.

76. Ibid.

77. E. J. Graff, "The Nation: How Dead Is DOMA, Really?" NPR, February 28, 2011, www.npr.org/2011/02/28/134127814/the-nation-how-dead-is-doma-really.

78. Nina Totenberg, "U.S. Sends Conflicting Signals on Gay Marriage Law," NPR, March 1, 2011, www.npr.org/2011/03/01/134132526/u-s-defends-doma-despite-dropping-support.

79. Brian Doherty, "Bob Barr Recants DOMA Very Publicly, a Couple of Months after Two Relevant Votes," *Reason*, January 5, 2009.

80. "AFA Attorney Pat Vaughn Tells Ed Vitagliano that DOMA Is Unconstitutional," *On Top Magazine*, March 1, 2011, www.ontopmag.com/article.aspx?id=7693&MediaType=1&Category=26.

81. The AP-National Constitution Center Poll, August 2011.

82. "Public Opinion and the Defense of Marriage Act," Human Rights Campaign Fund, www.hrc.org/domapoll2011.

83. Ibid.

84. Ibid.

85. Ibid.

86. Chris Johnson, "Couples Make History Testifying against DOMA," *Washington Blade*, July 22, 2011, www.washingtonblade.com/2011/07/20/senate-panel-hears-testimony-on-doma-repeal.

87. Ibid.

88. Ibid.

89. Tom Allison, "Marriage Equality Opponents Risk Hurting Republicans," Equality Matters, February 25, 2011, http://equalitymatters.org/blog/201102250010.

90. Matt Cover, "Republican Congressman Seeks to Protect Defense of Marriage Act in Court: Says Obama 'Not Adequately' Defending Law," CNSNews.com, October 12, 2010, http://cnsnews.com/news/article/republican-congressman-seeks-protect-defense-marriage-act-court-says-obama-not.

91. Tom Allison, "Marriage Equality Opponents Risk Hurting Republicans."

92. Ibid.

93. Whitney Pitcher, "Governor Palin Denounces President Obama's DOMA Decision," Free Republic, March 1, 2011, www.freerepublic.com/focus/f-news/2682002/posts.

94. Ibid.

95. Honorable Abner J. Mikva, Counsel to President Bill Clinton, "Presidential Authority to Decline to Execute Unconstitutional Statutes," November 2, 1994.

96. "Would Herman Cain Have Impeached Reagan, Both Bushes, and Clinton?" Equality Matters, August 18, 2011, http://equalitymatters.org/fact check/201108180009.

97. Ibid.

98. Ibid.

99. Ibid.

100. Damon W. Root, "Does Federal Law Trump an Oath to the Constitution?" Reason.com, March 2, 2011, http://reason.com/archives/2011/03/02/does-federal-law-trump-an-oath.

101. Damon W. Root, "More on Obama, Gay Marriage, and Executive Power," Reason.com, February 25, 2011, http://reason.com/blog/2011/02/25/more-on-obama-gay-marriage-and.

102. Ibid.

103. See "Federal Marriage Amendment," Wikipedia, http://en.wikipedia.org/wiki/Federal_Marriage_Amendment.

104. Ibid.

105. Ibid.

106. Ibid.

107. Ibid.

108. See Polling Report, "Law and Civil Rights."

109. Ibid.

110. Ibid.

111. David Badash, "GOP Debate: Constitutional Ban on Same-Sex Marriage Wins Big," New Civil Rights Movement, June 14, 2011, http://thenewcivilrights movement.com/gop-debate-constitutional-ban-on-same-sex-marriage-wins-big/ dont-ask-dont-tell/2011/06/14/22085.

112. Ibid.

113. Sean Eldridge, "New York's Same-Sex Couples Are Not Out of the Woods Yet," *The Nation*, June 30, 2011, www.thenation.com/article/161766/ new-york%E2%80%99s-same-sex-couples-are-not-out-woods-yet.

114. Carolyn Lochhead, "S.F. Gay Married Couple Loses Immigration Battle," SFGate.com, August 9, 2011, http://articles.sfgate.com/2011-08-09/ bay-area/29866637_1_marriage-act-immigration-equality-immigration -benefits.

115. Carlos Maza, "DOMA Immigration Cases Create Balancing Act for Administration," Equality Matters, May 9, 2011, http://equalitymatters.org/blog/ 201105090010.

116. Kirk Semple, "U.S. Drops Deportation Proceedings against Immigrant in Same-Sex Marriage," *New York Times*, June 29, 2011, www.nytimes.com/ 2011/06/30/us/30immig.html.

117. Chris Hawley, "Gay Marriage May Lead to Adoption Boom," Associated Press, July 12, 2011.

118. Ibid.

119. "Florida Ends Ban on Gay, Lesbian Adoptions," CNN.com, October 22, 2010, http://edition.cnn.com/2010/US/10/22/florida.gay.adoptions/index .html?iref=allsearch.

120. Ibid.

121. Rob Moritz, "Judge Strikes Down Adoption Ban," *Arkansas News*, April 16, 2010, http://arkansasnews.com/2010/04/16/judge-strikes-down-adoption-ban.

122. See "LGBT Adoption," Wikipedia, http://en.wikipedia.org/wiki/ LGBT_adoption.

123. Ibid.

124. "Results of Some Studies," Religious Tolerance, www.religioustolerance .org/hom_pare2.htm; Sadie F. Dingfeld, "The Kids Are All Right," *American Psychological Association Monitor* 36, no. 11 (December 2005): 66.

125. Colbert King, "Same-Sex Marriage Isn't the Threat to African American Families," *Washington Post*, March 6, 2011, http://voices.washingtonpost.com/postpartisan/2011/03/same-sex_marriage_isnt_the_thr.html.

126. Ibid.

127. Ibid.

128. Ibid.

129. Ibid.

130. David Boaz, "Phony Solutions for Real Social Ills," *Los Angeles Times*, February 7, 2011, http://articles.latimes.com/2011/feb/07/opinion/la-oe-boaz-social-conservatives-20110207.

131. Ibid.

132. Ibid.

133. Ibid.

134. "Talking Points about Adoption and Gay Parenting," American Civil Liberties Union, http://gbge.aclu.org/parenting/talking-points-about-adoption-and-gay-parents.

135. See Religious Tolerance, "Results of Some Studies"; Sadie F. Dingfeld, "The Kids Are All Right."

136. See Polling Report, "Law and Civil Rights."

137. Ibid.

CHAPTER 4: THE THORNY ISSUE OF GAY MARRIAGE

1. Andrew Sullivan, "Here Comes the Groom," *New Republic*, August 28, 1989, www.tnr.com/article/79054/here-comes-the-groom?page=0%2C1.

2. See "Same-Sex Marriage in the United States," Wikipedia, http://en.wikipedia.org/wiki/Same-sex_marriage_in_the_United_States.

3. Ibid.

4. Ibid.

5. Ibid.

6. Nandini Jayakrishna and Jonathan Saltzman, "Mass. Is 1st to Fight US Marriage Law," Boston.com, July 9, 2009, www.boston.com/news/local/massachusetts/articles/2009/07/09/mass_to_challenge_us_marriage_law.

7. See "Divorce Rates by State: 1990, 1995, and 1999–2009," CDC, www.cdc.gov/nchs/data/nvss/divorce_rates_90_95_99-09.pdf.

8. See "Timeline of Major Events" at Wikipedia, "Same-Sex Marriage in the United States."

9. See "Archive for the 'Gay Marriage' Category," Volokh Conspiracy, http://volokh.com/category/gay-marriage.

10. See "Federal Marriage Amendment," SourceWatch, www.sourcewatch .org/index.php?title=Federal_Marriage_Amendment.

11. David Badash, "GOP Debate: Constitutional Ban on Same-Sex Marriage Wins Big," New Civil Rights Movement, June 14, 2011, http://thenewcivilrights movement.com/gop-debate-constitutional-ban-on-same-sex-marriage-wins-big/ dont-ask-dont-tell/2011/06/14/22085.

12. See Wikipedia, "Same-Sex Marriage in the United States."

13. Ibid.

14. See "Law and Civil Rights," Polling Report, www.pollingreport.com/ civil.htm, for a variety of the latest polls on same-sex marriage.

15. See Appendix 4: Categories of Statutory Provisions, GAO-04-353R Defense of Marriage Act, 16.

16. Ross Douthat, "The Marriage Ideal," *New York Times*, August 8, 2010, www.nytimes.com/2010/08/09/opinion/09douthat.html.

17. For a detailed history of the evolution of marriage, including the views of Martin Luther, see Jim Peron, "Marriage's Shifting Status . . . and Gay Marriage Today," ifeminists.net, July 16, 2009, www.ifeminists.net/e107_plugins/ content/content.php?content.513.

18. Ibid.

19. See "Loving v. Virginia," Wikipedia, http://en.wikipedia.org/wiki/ Loving_v._Virginia.

20. Gardiner Harris, "Out-of-Wedlock Birthrates Are Soaring, U.S. Reports," *New York Times*, May 13, 2009, www.nytimes.com/2009/05/13/health/ 13mothers.html.

21. Ibid.

22. U.S. Census Bureau, Families and Living Arrangements: Current Population Survey (CPS) Reports, "Table HH-1, Households by Type: 1940 to Present."

23. See Jeffrey M. Jones, "Americans' Opposition to Gay Marriage Eases Slightly," Gallup, May 24, 2010, www.gallup.com/poll/128291/Americans-Opposition-Gay-Marriage-Eases-Slightly.aspx.

24. See Frank Newport, "Americans Turn More Negative toward Same-Sex Marriage," Gallup, April 19, 2005, www.gallup.com/poll/15889/Americans -Turn-More-Negative-Toward-SameSex-Marriage.aspx.

25. See Linda Lyons, "U.S. Next Down the Aisle Toward Gay Marriage?" Gallup, July 22, 2003, www.gallup.com/poll/8881/US-Next-Down -Aisle-Toward-Gay-Marriage.aspx.

26. See Polling Report, "Law and Civil Rights," for a variety of recent polls on same-sex marriage.

27. Ibid.

28. Ibid.

29. See AP Polls at http://surveys.ap.org.

30. Ibid.

31. See Polling Report, "Law and Civil Rights," for a variety of the latest polls on same-sex marriage.

32. Ibid.

33. Ibid.

34. Ibid.

35. Steve Peoples, "NH Gay Marriage Push Highlights GOP Shift," Associated Press, November 24, 2011.

36. Bruce Nolan, "Gay Marriage Divides Evangelicals along Generation Gap," *Huffington Post*, September 7, 2011.

37. David Lauter, "Poll: Support for Gay Marriage Continues to Rise," *Los Angeles Times*, November 3, 2011.

38. David Badash, "Obama, Bush Pollsters: Rapid Bipartisan Support for Marriage Equality," New Civil Rights Movement, July 27, 2011, http://thenewcivilrightsmovement.com/obama-bush-pollsters-rapid-bipartisan-support-for-marriage-equality/politics/2011/07/27/24441.

39. Ibid.

40. Ibid.

41. Ibid.

42. Ibid.

43. "Married to Marriage: 62% of Americans Say It's One Man, One Woman, Nothing Else" (news release), Alliance Defense Fund, June 16, 2011, www.adfmedia.org/News/PRDetail/4914.

44. See Polling Report, "Law and Civil Rights."

45. Ibid.

46. Ibid.

47. "Survey—Committed to Availability, Conflicted about Morality: What the Millennial Generation Tells Us about the Future of the Abortion Debate and the Culture Wars," Public Religion Research Institute, June 9, 2011, http://publicreligion.org/research/2011/06/committed-to-availability-conflicted-about-morality-what-the-millennial-generation-tells-us-about-the-future-of-the-abortion-debate-and-the-culture-wars.

48. See "Gay Marriage Gains More Acceptance," Pew Research Center, October 6, 2010, http://pewresearch.org/pubs/1755/poll-gay-marriage-gains-acceptance-gays-in-the-military.

49. Ibid.

50. See "ABC News/*Washington Post* Poll: Gay Marriage," ABCNews.com, March 18, 2011, http://abcnews.go.com/images/Politics/1121a6%20Gay%20Marriage.pdf.

51. See "Survey—Majority of Americans Say They Support Same-Sex Marriage, Adoption by Gay and Lesbian Couples," Public Religion Research

Institute, May 19, 2011, http://publicreligion.org/research/2011/05/majority-of-americans-say-they-support-same-sex-marriage-adoption-by-gay-and-lesbian-couples.

52. For a philosophical case for same-sex marriage by three conservatives, see Rick Moran, "The Conservative Case for Gay Marriage," Rightwing Nuthouse, April 18, 2009, http://rightwingnuthouse.com/archives/2009/04/18/the-conservative-case-for-gay-marriage; Margaret Hoover, "My Fellow Conservatives, Think Carefully about Your Opposition to Gay Marriage," FoxNews.com, August 9, 2010, www.foxnews.com/opinion/2010/08/09/margaret-hoover-prop-gay-rights-marriage-conservatives-civil-rights; and "A Conservative Christian Case for Civil Same-Sex Marriage," Musings on Christianity, Homosexuality, & the Bible, November 19, 2000, www.musingson.com/ccCase.html.

53. See Polling Report, "Law and Civil Rights."

54. Ibid.

55. "Most Republicans Support Recognition for Gay Couples," Public Policy Polling, www.publicpolicypolling.blogspot.com, May 4, 2011.

56. See "Same-Sex Marriage, Civil Unions and Domestic Partnerships," National Conference of State Legislatures, July 14, 2011, www.ncsl.org/default.aspx?tabid=16430.

57. See Polling Report, "Law and Civil Rights."

58. Ibid.

59. "Same Sex Marriage Opposed Slightly But Huge Support for Civil Unions," Zogby.com, July 7, 2011.

60. William A. Galston, "The 2010 Midterm Elections Were about Ideology," Brookings, November 4, 2010, www.brookings.edu/opinions/2010/1104_ideology_galston.aspx.

61. See Polling Report, "Law and Civil Rights."

62. Ibid.

63. Will Wilkinson, "How Long Can Conservatives Oppose Gay Marriage?" *The Week*, November 6, 2009.

64. Jeffrey R. Lax and Justin H. Phillips, "Gay Rights in the States: Public Opinion and Policy Responsiveness," *American Political Science Review* 103, no. 3 (2009).

65. See "AmericaVotes2006," CNN, www.cnn.com/ELECTION/2006/pages/results/states/VA/I/01/epolls.0.html.

66. Tim Murphy, "Focus on the Family Head: 'We've Probably Lost' on Gay Marriage," *Mother Jones*, May, 23, 2011, http://motherjones.com/mojo/2011/05/focus-family-weve-lost-gay-marriage.

67. Adam Nagourney, "Signs G.O.P. Is Rethinking Stance on Gay Marriage," *New York Times*, April 29, 2009, www.nytimes.com/2009/04/29/us/politics/28web-nagourney.html.

68. William A. Galston, "The 2010 Midterm Elections Were about Ideology."

69. See www.cnn.com/ELECTION/2006/pages/results/states/VA/I/01/epolls.0.html.

70. Rosalind S. Helderman and Jon Cohen, "Virginians Are Almost Evenly Split on Gay Marriage, Post Poll Finds," *Washington Post*, May 9, 2011, www.washingtonpost.com/local/politics/virginians-are-almost-evenly-split-on-gay-marriage-post-poll-finds/2011/05/06/AFFtojcG_story.html.

71. Ibid.

72. Damon Root, "Conservatives v. Libertarians: The Debate over Judicial Activism Divides Former Allies," Reason.com, July 2010, http://reason.com/archives/2010/06/08/conservatives-v-libertarians/singlepage.

73. Antonin Scalia, *A Matter of Interpretation* (Princeton, NJ: Princeton University Press, 1998).

74. Damon Root, "Conservatives v. Libertarians: The Debate over Judicial Activism Divides Former Allies."

75. Ibid.

76. Ibid.

77. Ibid.

78. Ibid.

79. Robert Levy, "The Moral and Constitutional Case for a Right to Gay Marriage," *New York Daily News*, January 7, 2010, www.nydailynews.com/opinion/moral-constitutional-case-a-gay-marriage-article-1.461657.

80. Ted Olson, "The Conservative Case for Gay Marriage," *Newsweek*, January 9, 2010.

81. See closing arguments at "Perry Trial Closing Arguments Transcript," American Foundation for Equal Rights, www.afer.org/legal-filings/hearing-transcripts/perry-trial-closing-arguments-transcript.

82. Ibid.

83. Ibid.

84. Ibid.

85. See "Perry v. Schwarzenegger," Wikipedia, http://en.wikipedia.org/wiki/Perry_v._Schwarzenegger.

86. Clark Ruper, "Victory for Liberty & Equality in California," Students for Liberty, August 5, 2010, http://studentsforliberty.org/news/victory-for-liberty-equality-in-california.

87. Ibid.

88. See Dayvoe, "But . . . ," 2 Political Junkies, August 8, 2010, http://2politicaljunkies.blogspot.com/2010/08/but.html.

89. Donald Lathbury, "Orange County Register Opposes Prop 8!" California Majority Report, October 1, 2008, www.camajorityreport.com/index.php?module=articles&func=display&aid=3624&ptid=9.

90. John Avlon, "The Right Attacks Prop 8 Judge," Daily Beast, August 5, 2010, www.thedailybeast.com/articles/2010/08/05/judge-vaughn-walker-prop-8-judge-target-for-gay-marriage-foes.html.

91. Ibid.

92. "Census: More Than 130,000 'Married' Gay Couples in U.S.," Foxnews.com, September 27, 2011, www.foxnews.com/politics/2011/09/27/census-more-than-130000-married-gay-couples-in-us.

93. Abby Goodnough and John Schwartz, "Judge Topples U.S. Rejection of Gay Unions," *New York Times*, July 6, 2010, www.nytimes.com/2010/07/09/us/09marriage.html.

94. Sandhya Somashekhar, "Tea Party Groups Choose to Stand Mute on Same-Sex Marriage Ruling," *Washington Post*, July 13, 2010, www.washingtonpost.com/wp-dyn/content/article/2010/07/13/AR2010071301436.html.

CHAPTER 5: THE RISE, FALL, AND RESURRECTION OF THE MODERN CONSERVATIVE MOVEMENT

1. See "Classical Liberalism," Wikipedia, http://en.wikipedia.org/wiki/Classical_liberalism.

2. Ibid.

3. See "Declaration of Independence," Charters of Freedom, http://archives.gov/exhibits/charters/declaration_transcript.html.

4. Ibid.

5. Adam Smith, *The Wealth of Nations* (New York: Bantam Classics, 2003).

6. See Brian Doherty, *Radicals for Capitalism: A Freewheeling History of the Modern Libertarian Movement* (New York: Public Affairs, 2007).

7. Arthur Ekirch, *The Decline of American Liberalism* (Oakland, CA: Independence Institute, 2009).

8. Herbert Croly, *The Promise of American Life* (Boston: Northeastern University Press, 1989).

9. John Samples, *The Struggle to Limit Government: A Modern Political History* (Washington, DC: Cato Institute, 2010).

10. Ibid, 4.

11. Herbert Croly, *The Promise of American Life*, 4.

12. Garland S. Tucker III, *The High Tide of American Conservatism: Davis, Coolidge, and the 1924 Election* (Austin, TX: Emerald Books, 2010).

13. Thomas Sowell, *Economic Facts and Fallacies* (New York: Basic Books, 2007).

14. See Wikipedia, "Classical Liberalism."

15. Russell Kirk, *The Conservative Mind*, 7th ed. (Washington, DC: Regnery, 2001).

16. See "Conservatism in the United States," Wikipedia, http://en.wikipedia.org/wiki/Conservatism_in_the_United_States.

17. Ibid.

18. Ibid.

19. Ibid.

20. David Boaz, "Conservatives and Civil Rights, Then and Now," *Encyclopaedia Britannica Blog*, February 14, 2011, www.britannica.com/blogs/2011/02/conservatives-and-civil-rights-then-and-now.

21. US Government, Executive Order 10450, "Security Requirements for Government Employees," 1953.

22. Kenneth S. Wherry, "Report of the Investigations of the Junior Senator of Nebraska, a Member of the Subcommittee Appointed by the Subcommittee on Appropriations for the District of Columbia, on the Infiltration of Subversives and Moral Perverts into the Executive Branch of the United States Government," 1950.

23. Friedrich Hayek, *The Road to Serfdom* (Chicago: University of Chicago Press, 1994).

24. See "The Road to Serfdom," Wikipedia, http://en.wikipedia.org/wiki/The_Road_to_Serfdom.

25. Ibid.

26. For a fascinating overview of Robert Taft and the Old Right in the postwar period, see Murray Rothbard, "Swan Song of the Old Right," Ludwig von Mises Institute, June 21, 2011, http://mises.org/daily/2755.

27. Ayn Rand, *Atlas Shrugged* (New York: Random House, 1957).

28. For a detailed history of the libertarian part of the modern conservative movement, see Brian Doherty, *Radicals for Capitalism: A Freewheeling History of the Modern Libertarian Movement*.

29. Barry Goldwater, *Conscience of a Conservative* (Princeton, NJ: Princeton University Press, 2007).

30. See "Libertarianism in the United States," Wikipedia, http://en.wikipedia/wiki/Libertarianism_in_the_United_States.

31. Robert Nozick, *Anarchy, State, and Utopia* (New York: Basic Books, 1977).

32. See Ernest L. Ohlhoff, "Abortion: Where Do the Churches Stand?" Pregnant Pause, September 12, 2000, www.pregnantpause.org/people/wherchur .htm.

33. For the entire interview, see Manuel Klausner, "Inside Ronald Reagan," Reason.com, July 1975, http://reason.com/archives/1975/07/01/inside-ronald -reagan.

34. Ibid.

35. See Wikipedia, "Conservatism in the United States."

36. Scott Keeter, "Will White Evangelicals Desert the GOP?" Pew Research Center, May 2, 2006, http://pewresearch.org.

37. See Wikipedia, "Conservatism in the United States."

38. See "Contract with America," Wikipedia, http://en.wikipedia.org/wiki/ Contract_with_America.

39. See tonyfv, "Andrew Sullivan: Clinton Ran Anti-Gay Ads in 96," Daily Kos, March 11, 2008, www.dailykos.com/story/2008/03/11/464805/-Andrew -Sullivan:-Clinton-ran-anti-gay-ads-in-96.

40. David Boaz, "The Ohio 'Values Voters' Myth, Again," Cato@Liberty, October 11, 2006, www.cato-at-liberty.org/the-ohio-values-voters-myth-again.

41. See "Terri Schiavo Case," Wikipedia, www.wikipedia.org/wiki/ Terri_Schiavo_case.

42. "CNN.com Posted Misleading Graph Showing Poll Results on Schiavo Case," MediaMatters, March 22, 2005, http://mediamatters.org/research/ 200503220005.

43. Gary Langer, "Poll: No Role for Government in Schiavo Case," ABC News.com, March 21, 2005, http://abcnews.go.com/Politics/PollVault/story ?id=599622&page=1.

44. Ibid.

45. Michael Medved, "Will Conservatives Elect Obama Again?" Daily Beast, August 6, 2011, www.thedailybeast.com/articles/2011/08/06/obama-draws -support-from-conservatives-who-could-help-re-elect-him-in-2012.html.

46. CNN/*Time* Poll, October 14–15, 1998, at "Law and Civil Rights," Polling Report, www.pollingreport.com/civil.htm; *Newsweek* Poll, December 4–5, 2008, at Polling Report, "Law and Civil Rights"; CBS News Poll, August 20–24, 2010, at Polling Report, "Law and Civil Rights"; Lymari Morales, "Conservatives Shift in Favor of Openly Gay Service Members," Gallup, June 5, 2009, www.gallup.com/poll/120764/Conservatives-Shift-Favor-Openly-Gay -Service-Members.aspx.

CHAPTER 6: IS THE TEA PARTY NATION ANTI-GAY?

1. See "Rick Santelli's Shout Heard Round the World," CNBC, February 22, 2009, www.cnbc.com/id/29283701/Rick_Santelli_s_Shout_Heard_Round_the_World.

2. See, for example, Kate Zernike, "Tea Party Avoids Divisive Social Issues," *New York Times*, March 12, 2010, http://www.nytimes.com/2010/03/13/us/politics/13tea.html; Dick Morris, "The New Republican Right," *The Hill*, October 9, 2010, http://thehill.com/opinion/columnists/dick-morris/124885-the-new-republican-right.

3. See Lydia Saad, "Tea Partiers Are Fairly Mainstream in Their Demographics," Gallup, April 5, 2010, www.gallup.com/poll/127181/tea-partiers-fairly-mainstream-demographics.aspx.

4. Scott Clement, "Most in Poll See Growing Wealth Gap," *Washington Post*, November 9, 2011.

5. David Lightman, "Bush Is the Biggest Spender since LBJ," McClatchy Washington Bureau, October 23, 2007, www.mcclatchydc.com/2007/10/24/20767/bush-is-the-biggest-spender-since.html.

6. See Tony Katz, "Chris Matthews Hates the Tea Party (Anyone Shocked?)," PJMedia, May 17, 2011, http://pajamasmedia.com/tatler/2011/05/17/chris-matthews-hates-the-tea-party-anyone-shocked?.html; Matt Taibbi, "The Truth about the Tea Party: Matt Taibbi Takes Down the Far-Right Monster and the Corporate Insiders Who Created It," *Rolling Stone*, September 28, 2010.

7. Kate Zernike, "Tea Party Avoids Divisive Social Issues."

8. Ibid.

9. Matt Welch and Nick Gillespie, "The Declaration of Independents," *Reason*, August/September 2011.

10. Kate Zernike, "Tea Party Avoids Divisive Social Issues."

11. Ibid.

12. See chapter 4.

13. "CBS News/*New York Times* Poll: National Survey of Tea Party Supporters," *New York Times*, April 24, 2010, http://documents.nytimes.com/new-york-timescbs-news-poll-national-survey-of-tea-party-supporters?ref=politics.

14. "Survey—Religion and the Tea Party in the 2010 Election: An Analysis of the Third Biennial American Values Survey," Public Religion Research Institute, October 2010, http://publicreligion.org/research/2010/10/religion-tea-party-2010.

15. Ibid.

16. Ibid.

17. "The Tea Party, Religion, and Social Issues," Pew Forum on Religion & Public Life, February 23, 2011, http://pewresearch.org/pubs/1903/tea-party-movement-religion-social-issues-conservative-christian.

18. Pew Forum on Religion & Public Life, "The Tea Party, Religion, and Social Issues."

19. Public Religion Research Institute, "Religion and the Tea Party in the 2010 Election."

20. "Canvassing the Tea Party," *Washington Post*, October 24, 2010.

21. Sandhya Somashekhar, "Tea Party Groups Choose to Stand Mute on Same-Sex Marriage Ruling," *Washington Post*, July 13, 2010, www.washingtonpost.com/wp-dyn/content/article/2010/07/13/AR2010071301436.html.

22. Ibid.

23. Ibid.

24. Ibid.

25. Ibid.

26. Devin Dwyer, "Social Conservatives Vow Fight for Defense of Marriage Act," ABCNews.com, February 25, 2011, http://abcnews.go.com/Politics/social-conservatives-vow-defend-doma-pressure-obama/story?id=13000776.

27. Jesse Zwick, "Liberals More Divided over Defense of Marriage Act Ruling than Tea Partiers," Minnesota Independent, July 12, 2010, http://minnesotaindependent.com/61333/liberals-more-divided-over-defense-of-marriage-act-ruling-than-tea-partiers.

28. Jonathan Rauch, "Tea-Baggers in Texas," Independent Gay Forum, September 5, 2010, http://igfculturewatch.com/2010/09/05/tea-baggers-in-texas.

29. David Kirby and Emily Ekins, "The Tea Party's Other Half," Cato@Liberty, October 28, 2010, www.cato.org/pub_display.php?pub_id=12515.

30. Ibid.

31. Ibid.

32. James Hohmann, "Tea Partiers in Two Camps: Palin vs. Paul," *Politico*, April 19, 2010, www.politico.com/news/stories/0410/35988.html.

33. Ibid.

34. David Gibson, "Glenn Beck Says Gay Marriage 'No Threat' to America," Politics Daily, August 13, 2010, www.politicsdaily.com/2010/08/13/glenn-beck-says-gay-marriage-no-threat-to-america.

35. Clarence Page, "O'Donnell Was Right," *Chicago Tribune*, October 27, 2010, http://articles.chicagotribune.com/2010-10-27/news/ct-oped-1027-page-20101027_1_church-and-state-christine-o-donnell-separation.

36. *Corporate Equality Index 2011: Rating American Workplaces on LGBT Equality* (Washington, DC: Human Rights Campaign, October 4, 2010).

37. Joseph Farah, "The Great Tea-Party Debate Is On," WorldNetDaily, August 23, 2010, www.wnd.com/?pageId=168737.

38. Ibid.

39. "The Hostile Takeover," *TIA Daily*, August 23, 2010, www.intellectual activist.com/tiaDaily.html.

40. "Sarah Palin's 'Christian Nation' Remarks Spark Debate," ABCNews .com, April 20, 2010, http://abcnews.go.com/Politics/sarah-palin-sparks-church -state-separation-debate/story?id=10419289.

41. Gene Healy, "Was It a 'Church Picnic' or a Freedom Rally?" *Washington Examiner*, August 31, 2010.

42. Ibid.

43. Ben Smith and Byron Tau, "GOP Is Urged to Avoid Social Issues," *Politico*, November 14, 2010, www.politico.com/news/stories/1110/45110.html.

44. Ibid.

45. Killian Melloy, "Tea Party Faction Rejects GOProud's Plea for Inclusion," *Edge*, November 23, 2010, www.edgeboston.com/index.php?ch=news& sc=&sc2=features&sc3=category_link&id=113249&pg=2.

46. "The Marriage Vow: A Declaration of Dependence upon Marriage and Family," The Family Leader, www.thefamilyleader.com/the-marriage-vow.

47. Ibid.

48. See "Gary Johnson Calls Family Leader Pledge 'Offensive and Unrepublican,'" *Truth for a Change Blog*, July 9, 2011, www.garyjohnson2012.com/gary-johnson-calls-family-leader-pledge-offensive-and-unrepublican.

49. Ibid.

50. Ibid.

51. Carlos Maza, "Half of the Tea Party Congress Supports Federal Intrusion into State Marriage Laws," Equality Matters, March 17, 2011, equalitymatters .org/blog/201103170003.

52. Margaret Talbot, "Obama, DOMA, and States' Rights," *New Yorker*, February 24, 2011.

CHAPTER 7: WHERE DO WE GO FROM HERE?

1. Bennett Roth, "Pro-Gay Groups Find New Allies in the GOP," *Roll Call*, September 22, 2010, www.rollcall.com/issues/56_28/-50098-1.html.

2. Marc Ambinder, "Bush Campaign Chief and Former RNC Chair Ken Mehlman: I'm Gay," *Atlantic*, August 2010, www.theatlantic.com/politics/archive/2010/08/bush-campaign-chief-and-former-rnc-chair-ken-mehlman-im-gay/62065.

3. Perry Bacon Jr., "The GOP's Dilemma: Winning over Gay Rights Advocates Could Mean Losing Part of Its Base," *Washington Post*, September 28, 2010.

4. Bennett Roth, "Pro-Gay Groups Find New Allies in the GOP."

5. Todd J. Gilman, "Excused Absence: NRCC Chair Pete Sessions Skips Gay/Lesbian GOP Dinner, but Group Shrugs It Off as a Scheduling Conflict," *Dallas Morning News*, September 22, 2010.

6. See "LGBT Rights in the United States," Wikipedia, http://wikipedia.org/wiki/LGBT_rights_in_the_United_States.

7. Jon Henke, "CPAC 2010: The GOProud Controversy," Next Right, December 29, 2009, http://thenextright.com/jon-henke/cpac-2010-the-goproud-controversy.

8. Zaid Jilani, "CPAC Conference Dissolves into Right-Wing Civil War over Gay Rights," Think Progress, February 19, 2010, http://thinkprogress.org/politics/2010/02/19/83048/cpac-conference-dissolves-into-right-wing-civil-war-over-gay-rights.

9. Ibid.

10. Jennifer Rubin, "A Response to the CPAC Boycotters," *Washington Post*, January 12, 2011, http://voices.washingtonpost.com/right-turn/2011/01/a_response_to_the_cpac_boycott.html.

11. Ibid.

12. Ibid.

13. See "Liberty Counsel May Lead Pullout of CPAC if Homosexual Group GOProud Remains as Co-Sponsor," Americans for Truth about Homosexuality, http://americansfortruth.com/2009/12/15/liberty-counsel-may-lead-pullout-of-cpac-if-homosexual-group-goproud-remains-as-co-sponsor.

14. "Gay GOP Group Barred from Sponsoring CPAC," *Washington Blade*, August 4, 2011, http://www.washingtonblade.com/2011/08/02/gay-gop-group-barred-from-sponsoring-cpac.

15. Matt Welch and Nick Gillespie, "The Declaration of Independents," *Reason*, August/September 2011.

16. Ibid.

17. Lydia Saad, "In 2010, Conservatives Still Outnumber Moderates, Liberals," Gallup, June 25, 2010, www.gallup.com/poll/141032/2010-conservatives-outnumber-moderates-liberals.aspx.

18. Ibid.

19. Matt Welch and Nick Gillespie, "The Declaration of Independents."

20. Ibid.

21. Ronald Brownstein, "The Age of Volatility," *National Journal*, October 29, 2011.

22. Dan Balz, "Will Demographic Shifts Save Obama in 2012?" *Washington Post*, November 27, 2011, www.washingtonpost.com/politics/will-demographic-shifts-save-obama-in-2012/2011/11/26/gIQAn8h7yN_story.html.

23. Ibid.

CHAPTER 8: A LAST HURRAH FOR REPUBLICAN ANTI-GAY BIGOTRY?

1. See the American Family Association website (www.afa.net).

2. See "Bryan Fischer," Right Wing Watch, www.rightwingwatch.org/category/individuals/bryan-fischer; Erik Eckholm, "With Rally, Christian Group Asserts Its Presence in '12 Race," *New York Times*, August 2, 2011, www.nytimes.com/2011/08/04/us/politics/04family.html.

3. Ibid.

4. Ibid.

5. Ibid.

6. Ibid.

7. Ibid.

8. Ibid.

9. Ibid.

10. Ibid.

11. Ibid.

12. "Perry's Association with Hate Groups Nothing New," Dallasvoice.com, June 28, 2011, www.dallasvoice.com/perrys-association-hate-groups-1081493.html.

13. Ibid.

14. Ibid.

15. Ibid.

16. David Badash, "MSNBC Positions Anti-Gay Hate Group Head Tony Perkins as Values Leader," New Civil Rights Movement, October 13, 2011, http://thenewcivilrightsmovement.com/msnbc-positions-anti-gay-hate-group-head-tony-perkins-as-values-leader/politics/2011/10/13/28459.

17. Ibid.

18. Nick Wing, "Tony Perkins: Gay Teens Resort to 'Depression or Suicide' because They Know They're 'Abnormal,'" *Huffington Post*, October 27, 2010, www.huffingtonpost.com/2010/10/27/tony-perkins-gay-teen-suicide_n_774580.html.

19. See the State of Belief website (http://stateofbelief.com).

20. Liz Essley, "Credo: Tony Perkins," *Washington Examiner*, August 21, 2011, http://washingtonexaminer.com/local/2011/08/tony-perkins.

21. Ibid.

22. See "Where Does Republican Candidate Rick Perry Stand on Social Issues?" Wintery Knight, August 16, 2011, http://winteryknight.wordpress.com/2011/08/16/where-does-republican-candidate-rick-perry-stand-on-social-issues.

23. Carlos Maza, "Rick Perry Makes Up with Anti-Gay Groups: 'Obviously, Gay Marriage Is Not Fine with Me,'" Equality Matters, July 28, 2011, http://politicalcorrection.org/blog/201107280009.

24. Ibid.

25. Paul Bowers, "Perry Wants to Bring Back Don't Ask Don't Tell, School Prayer," *Charleston City Paper*, December 8, 2011.

26. See "Mitt Romney on Civil Rights," On the Issues, www.ontheissues.org/2012/Mitt_Romney_Civil_Rights.htm.

27. Ibid.

28. Ibid.

29. Ibid.

30. Ibid.

31. Fred Lucas, "Romney Says He Supports 'Partnership Agreements' for Same-Sex Couples," CNSNews.com, October 11, 2011, http://cnsnews.com/news/article/romney-says-he-supports-partnership-agreements-same-sex-couples.

32. Igor Volsky, "Romney to Nashua Telegraph: 'I Favor Gay Rights,'" Think Progress, November 21, 2011, http://thinkprogress.org/lgbt/2011/11/21/373570/romney-to-nashua-telegraph-i-favor-gay-rights.

33. Brian Montopoli, "Mitt Romney Pledges Opposition to Gay Marriage," CBSNews.com, August 4, 2011, www.cbsnews.com/8301-503544_162-20088274-503544.html.

34. "NOM Speaker Blames East Coast Earthquake on Gays," Raw Story, August 24, 2011, www.rawstory.com/rawreplay/2011/08/nom-speaker-blames-east-coast-earthquake-on-gays.

35. Ibid.

36. Ryan Lizza, "Leap of Faith," *New Yorker*, August 15, 2011.

37. Ibid.

38. Ibid.

39. David Badash, "Michele Bachmann's Top Ten Anti-Gay Quotes," New Civil Rights Movement, June 2, 2011, http://thenewcivilrightsmovement.com/michele-bachmanns-top-ten-anti-gay-quotes/politics/2011/06/02/21233.

40. Ibid.

41. Ibid.

42. Ibid.

43. Alexander Burns, "Bachmann: Natural Disasters a Warning to D.C.," *Politico*, August 29, 2011, www.politico.com/news/stories/0811/62217.html.

44. See "Michele Bachmann on Civil Rights," On the Issues, www.ontheissues.org/House/Michele_Bachmann_Civil_Rights.htm.

45. Ibid.

46. "Ron Paul on Civil Rights," On the Issues, www.ontheissues.org/2012/Ron_Paul_Civil_Rights.htm.

47. Ibid.

48. Ibid.

49. Ibid.

50. Doug Mataconis, "Ron Paul Gets It Wrong on DOMA," United Liberty, February 28, 2011, www.unitedliberty.org/articles/7801-ron-paul-gets-it-wrong-on-doma.

51. David Badash, "The 15 House Republicans (Yes, Republicans) Who Voted to Repeal Don't Ask, Don't Tell," New Civil Rights Movement, December 15, 2010, http://thenewcivilrightsmovement.com/the-15-house-republicans-yes-republicans-who-voted-to-repeal-dont-ask-dont-tell/dont-ask-dont-tell/2010/12/15/16221.

52. See "Ron Paul on Crime," On the Issues, www.ontheissues.org/2012/Ron_Paul_Crime.htm.

53. See Kyle Mantyla, "Fischer: Unlike President Obama, Herman Cain Is 'Authentically Black,'" Right Wing Watch, May 23, 2011, www.rightwingwatch.org/print/7407.

54. See "Herman Cain on Crime," On the Issues, www.ontheissues.org/2012/Herman_Cain_Crime.htm.

55. Ibid.

56. Ibid.

57. Ibid.

58. Ryan J. Foley, "Testimony: Cain Campaign Concealed Gay Aide's Role," Associated Press, September 14, 2011.

59. See On the Issues, "Herman Cain on Crime."

60. Stuart Taylor, "Santorum on Sex: Where the Slippery Slope Leads," *Atlantic*, May 6, 2003.

61. David Boaz, "Rick Santorum and Limited Government," Cato@Liberty, December 9, 2009, www.cato-at-liberty.org/rick-santorum-and-limited-government.

62. See "Rick Santorum on Civil Rights," On the Issues, www.ontheissues.org/2012/Rick_Santorum_Civil_Rights.htm.

63. Ibid.

64. Ibid.

65. Ibid.

66. Ibid.

67. See Elon Green, "A Timeline of Tim Pawlenty's Evolving Homophobia," Think Progress, February 9, 2011, http://thinkprogress.org/politics/2011/02/09/143203/timeline-pawlenty-gays.

68. Ibid.

69. Ibid.

70. Ibid.

71. Ibid.

72. Ibid.

73. Kendra Marr, "Tim Pawlenty to Sign NOM Marriage Pledge," *Politico*, August 5, 2011, www.politico.com/news/stories/0811/60763.html.

74. Igor Volsky, "Pawlenty: Rescinding Funds to Implement DADT Repeal Is 'A Reasonable Step,'" Think Progress, February 7, 2011, thinkprogress.org/lgbt/2011/02/07/177247/pawlenty-dadt-2-2.

75. Kendra Marr, "Tim Pawlenty to Sign NOM Marriage Pledge."

76. "Gingrich: I'd Stop Gay Rights Progress," Advocate.com, www.advocate.com/News/Daily_News/2011/03/28/Gingrich_Id_Stop_Gay_Rights_Progress.

77. Ibid.

78. See "Newt Gingrich on Civil Rights," On the Issues, www.ontheissues.org/2012/Newt_Gingrich_Civil_Rights.htm.

79. Ibid.

80. Ibid.

81. Ibid.

82. Lisa Keen, "Romney Signs NOM's Marriage Pledge," Keen News Service, August 9, 2011, www.keennewsservice.com/2011/08/09/romney-signs-noms-marriage-pledge.

83. Igor Volsky, "Gingrich Secured $200,000 for Iowa Judge Recall Campaign," Think Progress, March 3, 2011, http://thinkprogress.org/lgbt/2011/03/03/177284/gingrich-judges.

84. See "Jon Huntsman on Civil Rights," On the Issues, www.ontheissues.org/2012/Jon_Huntsman_Civil_Rights.htm; Ryan Watkins, "Former Utah Gov. Jon Huntsman Announces GOP Presidential Bid, Viewed as Moderate on Gay Issues," GA Voice, June 21, 2011, www.thegavoice.com/index.php/news/national-news/2833-former-utah-gov-jon-huntsman-announces-gop-presidential-bid-viewed-as-moderate-on-gay-issues.

85. Ibid.

86. Tom Head, "Jon Huntsman on Civil Liberties," About.com, http://civilliberty.about.com/od/profiles/p/Jon-Huntsman-Civil-Liberties.htm.

87. Ibid.

88. Lisa Keen, "Romney Signs NOM's Marriage Pledge."

89. See "Gary Johnson Calls Family Leader Pledge 'Offensive and Unrepublican,'" *Truth for a Change Blog*, July 9, 2011, www.garyjohnson2012.com/gary-johnson-calls-family-leader-pledge-offensive-and-unrepublican.

90. Lucy Steigerwald, "Gary Johnson Comes Out in Favor of Gay Marriage," Reason.com, December 2, 2011.

91. See "Gary Johnson on Civil Rights," On the Issues, www.ontheissues.org/2012/Gary_Johnson_Civil_Rights.htm.

92. See "Conservatives on LGBT Issues: By Candidate," Center for American Progress Action Fund, February 22, 2011, www.americanprogressaction.org/issues/2011/03/pdf/lgbtissues-bycandidate.pdf.

INDEX

ABOUT THE AUTHOR

David Lampo is the publications director at the Cato Institute in Washington, DC, and a longtime Republican and libertarian activist. He serves as vice president of the Log Cabin Republican Club of Virginia and was a Republican precinct captain in Fairfax County, Virginia, for eight years. He is the author of numerous op-eds that have appeared in such publications as the *Washington Post, Chicago Tribune, Newsday, Richmond Times-Dispatch, Sacramento Bee, San Jose Mercury News, Albuquerque Tribune, National Review Online, Libertarian Review,* and *Inquiry*.